Living with lodgers

Manchester University Press

Living with lodgers

Household economy and social
relations in working-class
Victorian England

Vicky Holmes

MANCHESTER UNIVERSITY PRESS

The right of Vicky Holmes to be identified as the author of this work has been asserted in accordance with the Copyright, Designs and Patents Act 1988.

Published by Manchester University Press
Oxford Road, Manchester, M13 9PL

www.manchesteruniversitypress.co.uk

British Library Cataloguing-in-Publication Data
A catalogue record for this book is available from the British Library

ISBN 978 1 5261 7028 6 hardback

First published 2025

The publisher has no responsibility for the persistence or accuracy of URLs for any external or third-party internet websites referred to in this book, and does not guarantee that any content on such websites is, or will remain, accurate or appropriate.

Typeset
by Deanta Global Publishing Services, Chennai, India

Contents

Figures

Acknowledgements

I have lived with lodgers for perhaps more years than I care to acknowledge. Having stumbled across them when I first delved into coroners' inquests back in 2007 during a study of fatal household accidents, I found those particular lodgers a home in the *Journal of Victorian Culture* in 2014. Following this publication, my focus veered to the Victorian marital bed: I was not wholly unsurprised to find lodgers slumbering nearby, but I was somewhat disconcerted to find some under its sheets. In 2020, I finally settled down to research a book dedicated solely to lodgers and those with whom they lived. Then the pandemic hit. So while I spent many hours of the lockdowns crafting a range of vehicles from cardboard to entertain a two-year-old stuck at home, Ruth Mather and Jackie Reed trawled through nineteenth-century newspapers in search of lodgers – I am indebted to their assistance during this time. I am also eternally grateful to all those who laboured behind the scenes of various digitisation projects. Without the British Newspaper Archives, Findmypast, and the Integrated Census Microdata (I-CeM) Project, such a project of this scale would not have been possible and certainly not during the disruption of the past few years.

This book would also not have been possible without the support networks formed online amid the pandemic. I would like to thank the early morning writing group of Cathy Mazak's Momentum programme and the Friday regulars of the Women's History Network online writing retreat for taking the writing process beyond the solitary endeavour. However, there are insufficient words when it comes to thanking Helen Sword and the members of the Live

Writing Studio for their continued support, enthusiasm for the project, and fabulous feedback over the past two years – any prepositional podge the reader might come across is entirely of my own hand.

I would also like to thank Lyndon Moore for his support and guidance during the early stages of the project, as well as Joe Harley for his always helpful feedback on introductions, along with Simon Dyson, Eddy Higgs, and Gillian Williamson (who has also found herself living with landlords and lodgers) for their meticulous reading of the final draft. Many thanks also to the anonymous reader for Manchester University Press for their similarly meticulous reading and support of the book; the list of page/line numbers pertaining to typos was much appreciated. And, finally, I would like to thank my editors at Manchester University Press, Meredith Carroll and Humairaa Dudhwala, for always providing prompt answers to my questions and for helping me over any bumps in the road.

Research for this book has been financially assisted by the Women's History Network Early Career Fellowship.

Abbreviations

CEBs	Census Enumerators' Books
CLH	Common Lodging House
GRO	General Record Office
I-CeM	Integrated Census Microdata
TNA	The National Archives

Introduction

Trudging around England on the night of 5 April 1891, the General Record Office's (GRO) expansive army of census enumerators encountered over one million persons living as lodgers in private households.[1] This was not their first encounter with domestic dwelling lodgers. Ever since the GRO sought to establish the relationship with the head of household in the 1851 census, the lodger has made their presence known.[2] Yet despite their prevalence, aside from discussions about whether they should be categorised as lodgers (those who simply lodged) or boarders (those seated at the family table) – a delineation that does not appear to have concerned those involved – the GRO took little interest in these inhabitants beyond their counting.[3] Likewise, scholarship on the Victorian home has primarily overlooked this far-from-liminal figure in the domestic space. Throwing open the doors to the Victorian working-class home, where Michael Anderson established the majority of lodgers resided, and bringing the lodger out of the shadows, this book delves into their domestic arrangements. Exploring the lodger's place in the working-class home, from the point of arrival to their exit, the book uncovers much on household economics and social relations that have, until now, remained largely hidden from our view. Thus, not only does the book open up the world of the Victorian lodgers and the households that took them in, but it also reshapes our understanding of the working-class home.

England's population rapidly expanded in the Victorian period. In 1841, England's population totalled just 14,995,138. By 1901 – the year after the book concludes – it had more than doubled to

30,805,466.[4] Much of the growth was concentrated in England's large industrial towns and cities, putting pressure on its housing stock. A centuries-old solution to the need for housing was for some found by taking up lodgings. However, we would easily be forgiven for thinking that most of Victorian England's lodgers lived in common lodging houses (CLH). Dotted across the urban landscape, in London alone, at its peak in the 1850s, there were an estimated 3,300 CLHs – with low fees and a no-questions-asked policy – housing around fifty thousand nightly lodgers drawn from 'outcast' society.[5] Yet as rapidly as these overcrowded lodging houses appeared, so did the governing classes' concerns over them. Viewed as dens of immorality, crime, and disease, CLHs were, as Jane Hamlett states, 'increasingly invaded by legislation, the police, religious visitors, and "slummers"'. Indeed, 1851 saw the passing of the first Common Lodging House Act, the same year the GRO introduced the question regarding the relationship to the head of household in the census.[6] The consequence of these concerns and attempts of governance, alongside the appearance of the model lodging house, was the creation of a significant paper trail concerning these institutional dwellings throughout the Victorian period, most abundant being parliamentary papers, police reports, and slummers' accounts. Moreover, as Alison Kay's study of female-run lodging houses highlights, the keepers themselves – to protect their livelihood – left documentary evidence in the form of fire insurance records.[7] Consequently, the lodging-house lodger and their keepers have drawn much attention. However, domestic dwelling lodgings, where most lodgers laid their heads at night, have remained in obscurity.

Michael Anderson, one of the first historians to venture into Victorian England's domestic dwelling lodgings, weaves the lodger and lodgings into his broader discussion on family structure in mid-nineteenth-century Lancashire. Deriving his data from the census enumerators' books (CEBs), the books filled out by enumerators from which the GRO produced its statistics up until 1911, Anderson's work profiles lodgers and those households accommodating them in the booming cotton town of Preston, Lancashire.[8] Almost immediately, Anderson's findings upend our idea of who Victorian England's lodgers were, for among the migrant lodgers, Anderson reveals a significant number of non-migrant adolescents and young adults taking up lodgings in their hometown. Yet herein, Anderson highlights a considerable problem in using the CEBs to understand the lodgers and the households that took them in: the CEBs do not reveal why people took up lodgings or took in lodgers. Although Anderson was able to determine that non-migrant lodgers had no living parents in the town, he could only speculate that parental death was the cause of their move into lodgers. As I will demonstrate in Chapter 2, Anderson was not far off the mark here. However, as with life, death as a cause of a move into lodgings was a much more complicated picture.[9]

The most comprehensive work to date on Victorian lodgers and the householders that took them in was undertaken by Leonore Davidoff shortly after Anderson's 1871 study. Employing a range of sources, including the CEBs, Davidoff's exploration of lodgers and landladies is centred around the 'domestic ideal' and the blurred lines between home and work created by taking in lodgers. In this study, Davidoff, alongside tackling the definition of a lodger – a problem that, as noted above, vexed the Registrar General – provides valuable insight into the supply of and demand for lodgings, matters of payment and what was provided, and the complexities and sexual innuendos that abounded regarding the landlady–lodger relationship. Thus, Davidoff's work provides much of the framework for the present book. Yet as well as framing the bigger picture of lodging in this period, Davidoff turned to autobiographies and oral histories – as does Beatrice Moring's recent research on lodging in Finland – to provide glimpses into the individual experience of living as or with a lodger.[10] For example, Davidoff tells the story of an older man who, in the 1900s, escaped his drunken son with whom he was living by taking lodgings with the mother of eight children and paying her 2s. 6d. a week, along with giving her the produce from his greenhouse.[11] We have so much to glean from such individual stories presented in the sources, in this case, oral testimony. Although Davidoff uses this example to demonstrate flexibility in lodgings when it came to payment, we also learn the reasons that compelled this older man to seek lodgings – family discord – and, latterly, how he was provided with care as he declined, the women 'nurs[ing] him until he died'. Individual stories, as discussed below, are this book's backbone, coming from another source to which individual accounts from lodgers and the householders that took them in are in abundance. Yet since the publication of Davidoff's research in 1979 (and successive years), the domestic dwelling lodger and *his* lodgings have slipped from the historian's sight, except for those exploring – as discussed in Chapter 1 – household economies during this period.

Definitions, sources, and methodology

This book focuses not on the business enterprises that were the lodging houses of Victorian England but domestic dwellings – private residences – where lodgers were taken into the *home*. In particular, I focus on the tenanted homes of the Victorian working class, where lodgers were most prevalent during this period. In doing so, I also move away from the terms 'landlady' and 'landlord' to refer to those taking in lodgers, for, as will be seen, the lodgers themselves rarely refer to the people with whom they lodged as so, nor did the people taking them in. Instead, unless directed otherwise in the sources, I refer to those who took lodgers into their homes as 'householders'. The term 'lodger', however, remained in common parlance when it came to domestic dwellings. For those turning to the CEBs, there have always been two clear types of paying guests in the home – the *lodger*, one who pays for lodgings, and the *boarder*, one who pays for board and lodgings. Yet such a sharp delineation seemed only to concern the GRO. Moving beyond those relationships assigned by a stranger knocking at the door every ten years, I instead turn to the inhabitants therein to provide their own definition of the ties formed under their roof as will be discussed below. Not only does this reveal, as will be discussed at length in Chapter 2, the complex and often multilayered bonds between householders and their lodgers and boarders, but it also demonstrates that 'lodger' served as an all-encompassing term that – among the Victorian working class – not only included those who lodged but typically those who boarded as well. Therefore, following this trend, the term 'lodger' is used to describe both lodgers and boarders unless the said lodger is explicitly referred to as a boarder.

Working-class lodgers and the working-class householders accommodating them have left few direct personal accounts of their experiences.[12] To enter the world of Victorian domestic dwelling lodgings, we must look beyond the sources typically turned to for investigating this period and look to the sources and methods employed by historians of the long eighteenth century. Over the past two decades, a substantial amount of scholarship has been produced on eighteenth-century lodgers and their accommodation. For example, Amanda Vickery, John Styles, David Hussey and Margaret Ponsonby, and, most recently, Gillian Williamson have all opened the door – albeit, as Vickery notes, sometimes breaking the padlock first – onto the material and domestic world of lodgings in someone else's home.[13] Many of these historians turned to legal narratives to gain access to these people and their spaces, which, as Joanne McEwan notes in her research on the lodging exchange in the eighteenth century, skew towards 'points of conflict or tension' but nonetheless bring to light the 'social dynamics' and concerns over security, privacy, and choice that underpinned many lodging arrangements.[14] Indeed, Jane Hamlett's use of the Old Bailey Proceedings has transformed our understanding of the Victorian lodging house.[15] Crucially, as many of these works demonstrated, legal narratives also provide a voice to the generally unheard masses and unprecedented access to their home's interiors, both the material and social world of that space.

Following the example of eighteenth-century scholarship on lodgers and lodgings, I turn to court records for my evidence but shift the focus away from criminal proceedings. Across Victorian England, coroners' inquests were as ubiquitous as the domestic dwelling lodger. Investigating deaths that took place during times of tension (murders, suicides, etc.) and at points of monotony (accidental and other unexpected deaths), the coroner's courts throughout Victorian England made almost daily records of life behind closed doors, particularly for the working-class home, where concerns over domestic safety and hygiene promoted a skew toward investigating deaths under these roofs. Given the lodger's prevalence in the working-class home, they frequently appeared as either the deceased or a witness.

Coroners' inquests took place just hours after a death or the discovery of a body. In the larger metropolises, these proceedings were increasingly held in purpose-built coroner's courts, but, more often than not, an inquest was held at a convenient place not far from the site of death. Frequently, in the Victorian period, this was a local public house.[16] Having opened the inquest, the first task of the coroner and his jurors – comprising of at least twelve local men – was to view the body. While the moralising middle classes routinely found their way barred when attempting to enter the homes of the working class, the Victorian coroner and his court were granted unparalleled access to these homes, with the court frequently traversing these as part of their investigations.[17] In the case of domestic deaths, as I demonstrated elsewhere, the body was often viewed lying in situ.[18] Thus, as well as the viewing of the body in question, the coroner and his jurors would also comment on the deceased's surroundings for the record.

Returning to the site of the inquest, the questioning of witnesses commenced. Alongside those performing medical examinations of the body, medical practitioners who had attended to the deceased before death were called to give their account of any medical treatment they had provided and their opinion as to the cause of death, often detailing the domestic spaces and the environment's potential impact upon the health of the deceased.[19] Lay witnesses usually consisted of those present at the death and anyone else who could shed light upon events, from recalling mundane everyday domestic routines to being probed into divulging details of the most intimate nature.[20] Given the middle-class anxieties surrounding the encroachment of the lodger on the private household, as highlighted by Davidoff, it is unsurprising that when presented with a lodger, coroners' investigations would soon go off on a tangent. As will be observed throughout the book, the lodging inhabitants of the working-class domestic dwelling could find themselves being questioned on all manner of things, from their financial circumstances to their sexual relationships. All this was an imposition to those whose homes had been the scene of the domestic death but of great benefit to the historian, for not only do we see these homes through the lens of coroners, jurors, and medical witnesses, but we also hear the voices of the working class themselves – lodgers and householders – as their witness testimonies were transcribed for the record. However, there is one significant issue with using coroners' records: many of the original records of the Victorian coroner's courts no longer exist. Yet with the coroner's courts open to the public, sitting in the wings writing up the proceedings were members of the press, as can be seen in Figure 0.1 from George Sims's *Living London*

Figure 0.1 'A Coroner's Inquest' in George Robert Sims, *Living London* vol. I (1902), p. 315.

(1902). However, as noted prior, beyond the metropolis, such scenes would have been played out in a side room of a public house rather than a purpose-built courthouse.[21]

Death was a staple component of the Victorian press. Therefore, coroners' inquests provided gripping content to their middle-class readership, taking them into the world of the working-class home with reports of unnatural and, indeed, natural deaths.[22] Such journalism occasionally came under criticism, with critics referring to newspaper coverage of such proceedings as 'journalistic barbarism'. The deceased, they argued, was not spared any indignity as every aspect of their life and death was paraded in the press for 'curious and prying eyes'.[23] Nevertheless, the law of the marketplace prevailed. As a result, the historian is left with an extant record of these proceedings, with many reports even detailing both coroners' and witnesses' voices verbatim. Crucially, with the advent of digitisation, many inquest reports (as they hereafter will be referred to) are now accessible via the British Newspaper Library Archive.[24] In this book, with an abundance of newspapers at my fingertips via the British Newspaper Archive, I move away from the London-centric or regional focus on lodgers and the householders that accommodated them to provide a picture of lodgers and lodgings across England. Domestic dwelling lodgings were predominantly focused in urban areas. However, encompassing all of England, I also demonstrate that while rural lodgers were not as prevalent as their urban counterparts, their place in domestic dwellings was no less critical. However, it is essential to note here that while regional variations appear throughout the book, it is not my intention in the present book to focus on regional comparisons of lodgers and the households that took them in. Instead, I have taken a broad geographic area to ensure a representative view of domestic dwelling lodgings during this period.

Undertaking an online search of the British Library Newspaper Archive holdings of English newspapers – using the keywords 'lodger', 'boarder', and 'inquest' – selecting a sample every six years from 1840 to 1900 resulted in 895 inquest reports detailing domestic dwelling lodgings across England and their 1,098 lodgers. The inquest reports, however, are not used in isolation. Each inquest in my sample where names have been provided has been through the process of record linkage, as while the inquest reports provide a snapshot in time with some background information on individuals, additional sources – CEBs, other newspaper reports, along with birth, marriage, and death records – allowed me to corroborate the sampled inquest reports and in many cases provide further context on the individuals (householders and lodgers) coming before the coroner's courts. Of course, some of the householders and lodgers in my sample have evaded such data linkage, going unnamed in the inquest reports. For example, while an inquest held into the death of a householder provided their name and other details, if the lodger was not called as a witness – their presence alluded to in the testimonies of others – then they were not necessarily named, simply referred to a 'the lodger' or 'a lodger'. In total, 298 of the 1,098 lodgers remain nameless. Vice versa, the death of a lodger reveals at the very least their name, but alongside the unnamed householders, some female householders, even when providing testimony, evaded data linkage because the inquest report saw fit to only refer to them as 'Mrs' followed by their surname. Where an address was not given, identifying these women often proved an insurmountable task. As a consequence, I have been unable to identify 249 householders accommodating lodgers.

Book structure

My book follows the chronology of the domestic dwelling lodging arrangement, from the supply and demand of lodgings to the lodger's departure. In Chapter 1, 'The necessary lodger', we meet the Victorian working-class householders accommodating a lodger or lodgers. Taking in lodgers has long been seen as an economic activity undertaken by ageing widows. Yet as my chapter demonstrates, death does not explain the prevalent presence of lodgers in households headed by married persons in the inquest reports. Despite the argument that husbands 'crowded out' the option of a lodger during hard times, by the Victorian period, a significant deficiency in the breadwinner wage – whether through their own actions or matters beyond their control – left many with little choice but to accommodate a lodger. Although, for some, as will be seen, the purpose of a lodger was not necessarily for direct financial income but rather to provide the means – in the form of childcare – for women to go out to work. Chapter 1 also builds upon our understanding of the female-headed household necessity for a lodger. As well as looking more closely at the widow's story, I also examine the experiences of those deserted wives accommodating lodgers. Notably, the spinster taking in lodgers is inconspicuous in the chapter, suggesting they sit largely outside the working-class category. My chapter, therefore, in distinguishing the wide range of households accommodating lodgers, presents a better understanding of the financial predicaments and other motivations driving the lodger's presence in the home.

Chapter 2, 'The necessity for lodgings', moves on to meet the domestic dwelling lodgers of Victorian England. The stereotype of the Victorian lodger is that of the young single male, often having arrived in a place searching for work and lodgings. Expanding our understanding of the working-class Victorians taking up lodgings, I explore the various types of persons – male and female – and their motives for seeking lodgings. As with Anderson and the census, the inquest reports reveal numerous instances of non-migrants living in lodgings. Yet non-migrant lodgers are not just drawn from the young and single population but a broad spectrum of working-class persons. Using the inquest reports to divulge why non-migrants moved into lodgings, I demonstrate that while death was at the crux of many such moves, there was often a much more complex story of non-migrants' and migrants' motivations for taking up lodgings. Furthermore, while domestic dwelling lodgings were, for most, a temporary living arrangement, the inquest reports reveal some of those among the Victorian working class for whom lodgings were a perpetual way of life.

Having established the supply and demand for domestic dwelling lodgings, Chapter 3, 'The lodging exchange', connects these previous chapters by examining the process of finding lodgings and the economic exchanges between householder and lodger. Moving away from the idea of the stranger – in any sense of the word – I demonstrate that connections in the working-class community were the key to finding both lodgings and lodgers. In fact, the householder–lodger relationship usually began beyond the front door, whether in the workplace, the neighbourhood, or with one's kin. I then examine the lodging exchange – the arrangements between householders and lodgers regarding how much and how lodgers paid and what they would expect in return. In doing so, as well as highlighting distinct gender differences in the lodging arrangement, I demonstrate that lodging in someone else's home was often about much more than a simple exchange of money for bed and board. Indeed, it was not always a monetary exchange. Advancing the work of historians such as Beverley Lemire, I reveal the extent to which 'informal currencies' – in this case, the exchange of services – formed the basis of many lodging agreements.

Chapter 4, 'Compromised spaces?' moves further inwards into these domestic dwelling lodgings, asking to what extent taking in lodgers compromised the working-class household domestic space. Having gained entrance through the front door, lodgers – with few exceptions – became wholly entangled in day-to-day life within the household. Not only did households and lodgers eat together, but they also socialised together both inside and outside the home. Yet as the day drew to its close, distinct lines – except for where the fabric of the home prevented it – were drawn in the householder–lodger relationship. Aside from the cases where a female lodger was squeezed into the family's sleeping arrangements or where sleeping arrangements were realigned to accommodate a male lodger, most householders and their families retired to bed in their own room – whether it be the parlour or the bedroom – separate from that of their lodgers. However, lodgers – especially male lodgers – could not expect to sleep alone. Not only did they find themselves sharing bedrooms with other male lodgers, but they could also find themselves tussling for the sheets as they bedded down together for the night. Yet they often fared better than the family crammed into one bedroom or some of those lodgers sleeping alone.

Addressing the sexual narratives surrounding the lodging arrangement, Chapter 5, 'Beyond the boundaries', looks more intimately at the relationships that evolved between lodgers and householders. Music-hall songs and literary examples of the captivating widow preying upon her young, sometimes heroic, male lodger, trapping him into matrimony, have dominated the story of the lodger and the landlady relationship. Yet the reality presented in the inquest reports tells quite a different story. In this chapter, I argue that many of the documented sexual relationships between widows and their lodgers were far from cases of female-led entrapment. Instead, the male lodger often appears as the pursuant of the generally cautious female householder, leading to reversed power dynamics and tensions in relationships that go beyond the boundaries. Moreover, I will also explore those relationships between wives and lodgers that crossed the platonic boundaries in this chapter. With concerns that taking a young male lodger – the seducer – into the marital home would soon lead to adultery, the inquest reports reveal that while adultery did take place, albeit not as frequently as suggested, it tended to occur in those homes where the marriage was already fractured by the events that led to the presence of a lodger under their roof.

Chapter 6, 'Notice to quit', brings the story of the domestic dwelling lodger and householder to a close, exploring the lives of householders and lodgers as they move on from the domestic dwelling lodging arrangement. Alongside the impact of death, I focus on the legality of ejecting a lodger. Despite the often informal appearance of the arrangements made between householders and lodgers throughout the book, there is evidence of clear understanding between the two parties of terminating the relationship through serving notice. In establishing this, I demonstrate a formality in the householder–lodger relationship and expectations surrounding behaviour that often left householders more vulnerable than their lodgers. Finally, the book's conclusion moves into the twentieth century and the decline of the lodger before asking whether the current financial and housing crisis is once again bringing lodgers into the home.

My book, then, provides the first comprehensive history of domestic dwelling lodgers and lodgings in Victorian England. Moving away from the existing methodologies, my research builds on and extends the current scholarship on the lodger and lodgings and provides a new narrative as to the identity of the Victorian lodger, who took in lodgers and why, the financial and social exchanges between householders and lodgers, the negotiation and arrangement of domestic space, and the situations that led to blurred boundaries in these relationships. Through this, we gain an exhaustive understanding of social and economic life behind the closed doors of the Victorian working-class home through the observers and the individuals who lodged and who took in lodgers.

Notes

1 Lodgers and boarders accounted for nearly 7 per cent of those enumerated on private household schedules. Search details: 1891 census > England > Type of dwelling: Private Household Schedule > Residential inmates. [Residential inmates – Boarder (487,972) Residential inmates – Lodger (365,670) Residential inmates – Boarders' families (109,212) Residential inmates – Lodgers' families (90,739). Kevin Schürer and Edward Higgs, Integrated Census Microdata (I-CeM), 1851–1911. [data collection]. UK Data Service. SN: 7481 (2020). DOI: 10.5255/UKDA-SN-7481-2.

2 For a comprehensive history of the development of the Victorian census, see Edward Higgs, *Making Sense of the Census Revisited* (London: HMSO, 2005).

3 To the GRO, the lodger was seen as a separate entity from those with whom they lodged. A boarder was one who shared the same table. Yet in common parlance, both were generally referred to as lodgers.

4 Census of Great Britain, 1841, Enumeration Abstract, BPP 1843 XXII (496) 459; Census of England and Wales, 1901, BPP 1901 XC [Cd.616] 3. During this time, inhabited houses in England also grew from 2,755,710 in 1841 to 5,916,840 in 1891. www.histpop.org (accessed 21 December 2023).

5 Tom Crook, 'Accommodating the Outcast: Common Lodging Houses and the Limits of Urban Governance in Victorian and Edwardian

London', *Urban History*, 35:3 (2008), 414–36. DOI: 10.1017/ S0963926808005713; Jane Hamlett, *At Home in the Institution: Material Life in Asylums, Lodging Houses and Schools in Victorian and Edwardian England* (Basingstoke: Palgrave Macmillan, 2015), pp. 111–22.

6 Hamlett, *At Home in the Institution*, pp. 111–13.
7 Alison C. Kay, 'A Little Enterprise of Her Own: Lodging-House Keeping and the Accommodation Business in Nineteenth-Century London', *London Journal*, 28:2 (2003), 41–53. DOI: 10.1179/ldn.2003.28.2.41. More recently, Lesley Hoskins has explored the nineteenth-century lodging house through inventories in her examination of the intersection of home and work. Lesley Hoskins, 'Stories of Work and Home in the Mid-Nineteenth Century', *Home Cultures*, 8:2 (2011), 151–69. DOI: 10.2752/175174211X12961586699720.
8 Historians have long turned to the census by attempting to piece together the history of the domestic dwelling lodger and those who accommodate them. In the past fifty years, US and Canadian scholars have undertaken numerous census-based studies on boarders and boarding – a term more commonly used in the regions – in the nineteenth and early twentieth centuries: John Modell and Tamara K. Hareven, 'Urbanization and the Malleable Household: An Examination of Boarding and Lodging in American Families', *Journal of Marriage and Family*, 35:3 (1973), 467–79. DOI: 10.2307/350582; Bettina Bradbury, 'Pigs, Cows, and Boarders: Non-Wage Forms of Survival Among Montreal Families, 1861–1891', *Labour/Le Travail*, 14 (1984), 9–48; Sheva Medjuck, 'The Importance of Boarding for the Structure of the Household in the Nineteenth Century: Moncton, New Brunswick, and Hamilton, Canada West', *Histoire Sociale/Social History* 13 (1980), 207–13; Mark Peel, 'On the Margins: Lodgers and Boarders in Boston, 1860–1900', *The Journal of American History*, 72:4 (1986), 813–34. DOI: 10.2307/1908892; Richard Harris, 'The End Justifies the Means: Boarding and Rooming in a City of Homes, 1890–1951', *Journal of Social History*, 26 (1992), 331–58. DOI: 10.1353/jsh/26.2.331; Richard Harris, 'The Flexible House: The Housing Backlog and the Persistence of Lodging, 1891–1951', *Social Science History*, 18 (1994), 31–53. DOI: 10.1017/S0145553200021441; Peter Baskerville, 'Familiar Strangers: Urban Families with Boarders, Canada, 1901', *Social Science History*, 25:3 (2001), 321–46. DOI: 10.1017/S0145553200012141; Wendy Gamber, 'Away from Home: Middle-Class Boarders in the Nineteenth-Century City', *Journal of Urban History*, 31:3 (2005), 289–305. DOI: 10.1177/0096144204272415; David T. Beito and Linda Royster Beito, 'The "Lodger Evil" and the Transformation of Progressive Housing

Reform, 1890–1930', *The Independent Review*, 20:4 (2016), 485–508. More recently, Ruth McManus and Jeff Meek have turned to the census, alongside other sources, in their investigations of lodging and boarding at the turn of the twentieth century in Dublin and Scotland, respectively. Ruth McManus, 'Dublin's Lodger Phenomenon in the Early Twentieth Century', *Irish Economic and Social History*, 45:1 (2018), 23–46. DOI: 10.1177/0332489318801622; Jeff Meek, 'Boarding and Lodging Practices in Early Twentieth-Century Scotland', *Continuity and Change*, 31:1 (2016), 79–100. DOI: 10.1017/S0268416016000084.

 9 Michael Anderson, *Family Structure in Nineteenth Century Lancashire* (Cambridge: Cambridge University Press, 1971), pp. 43–55, 64, 74, 101–2, 116–17, 124–32, 156–8.

10 Beatrice Moring, 'Gender, Class and Lodging in Urban Finland Around 1900', *Continuity and Change*, 31:1 (2016), 47–77. DOI: 10.1017/ S0268416016000102.

11 Leonore Davidoff, 'The Separation of Home and Work? Landladies and Lodgers in Nineteenth- and Twentieth-Century England', in Sandra Burman (ed.), *Fit Work for Women* (London: Croom Helm, 1979), pp. 64–97; Leonore Davidoff, *Worlds Between: Historical Perspectives on Gender and Class* (Cambridge: Polity Press, 1995), pp. 151–79; Leonore Davidoff, Megan Doolittle, Janet Fink, and Katherine Holden, *The Family Story: Blood, Contract, and Intimacy, 1830–1960* (London: Longman, 1999). The example discussed is from Davidoff et al., *The Family Story*, p. 179.

12 Recent work undertaken by Emma Griffin and Rebecca Preston and Lesley Hoskins, using autobiographies, have provided glimpses of the Victorian and Edwardian lodger through the childhood gaze. Emma Griffin, *Bread Winner: An Intimate History of the Industrial Revolution* (New Haven, CT: Yale University Press, 2020). Lesley Hoskins and Rebecca Preston, 'Chickens, Ducks, Rabbits, and Me Dad's Geraniums: The Use and Meaning of Yards, Gardens and Other Outside Spaces of Urban Working-Class Homes', in Joseph Harley, Vicky Holmes, and Laika Nevalainen (eds), *The Working Class at Home, 1790–1940* (Cham: Palgrave Macmillan, 2022), pp. 145–69.

13 There is an expansive and continual body of literature on lodgers and their lodgings in the long eighteenth century. S. J. Wright, 'Sojourners and Lodgers in a Provincial Town: The Evidence from Eighteenth-Century Ludlow', *Urban History*, 17 (1990), 14–35. DOI: 10.1017/S0963926800014334; John Styles, 'Lodging at the Old Bailey: Lodgings and Their Furnishing in Eighteenth-Century London', in John Styles and Amanda Vickery (eds), *Gender, Taste and Material Culture in Britain and North America, 1700–1830*

(New Haven, CT: Yale University Press, 2006); Amanda Vickery, 'An Englishman's Home Is His Castle? Thresholds, Boundaries and Privacies in the Eighteenth-Century London House', *Past & Present*, 199:1 (2008), 147–73. DOI: 10.1093/pastj/gtn006; Alison Kay, '"It Buys Me Freedom": Genteel Lodging in Late-Seventeenth- and Eighteenth-Century London', *Parergon*, 24:2 (2007), 139–61. DOI: 10.3316/ielapa.200802523; and, most recently, Gillian Williamson, *Lodgers, Landlords and Landladies in Georgian London* (London: Bloomsbury Academic, 2021). The lodger and those taking in lodgers also appear within a number of texts pertaining to the long eighteenth-century home. Namely, Amanda Vickery, *Behind Closed Doors: At Home in Georgian England* (New Haven, CT: Yale University Press, 2009); Joanne McEwan and Pamela Sharpe (eds), *Accommodating Poverty: The Housing and Living Arrangements of the English Poor, c.1600–1850* (London: Palgrave Macmillan, 2011) – particular chapters: Joanne McEwan, 'The Lodging Exchange: Space, Authority and Knowledge in Eighteenth-Century London', in Joanne McEwan and Pamela Sharpe (eds), *Accommodating Poverty: The Housing and Living Arrangements of the English Poor, c.1600–1850* (London: Palgrave Macmillan, 2011), pp. 50–68 and Samantha K. Williams, '"I Was Forced to Leave My Place to Hide My Shame": The Living Arrangements of Unmarried Mothers in London in the Early Nineteenth Century', in *Accommodating Poverty*, pp. 191–218; David Hussey and Margaret Ponsonby, *The Single Homemaker and Material Culture in the Long Eighteenth Century* (Farnham: Ashgate, 2012).

14 McEwan and Sharpe, 'The Lodging Exchange', p. 51.

15 Hamlett, *At Home in the Institution*, pp. 111–59.

16 For more information, see Ian A. Burney, *Bodies of Evidence: Medicine and the Politics of the English Inquest, 1830–1926* (Baltimore, MD: Johns Hopkins University Press, 2000), pp. 80–106; Bernard V. Heathcote, *Viewing the Lifeless Body: A Coroner and His Inquests Held in Nottinghamshire Public Houses during the Nineteenth Century 1828 to 1866* (Nottingham: Nottinghamshire County Council, Culture & Community, 2006).

17 Through re-reading the threshold of the working-class home, Hewitt demonstrates that doors and windows – rather than falling wide open – were routinely secured and policed. Martin Hewitt, 'District Visiting and the Constitution of Domestic Space in the Mid-Nineteenth Century', in Janet Floyd and Inga Bryden (eds), *Domestic Space: Reading the Nineteenth-Century Interior* (Manchester: Manchester University Press, 1999), pp. 121–41.

18 Vicky Holmes, 'Dangerous Spaces: Working-Class Homes and Fatal Household Accidents in Suffolk, 1840–1900' (PhD thesis, University of Essex, 2012), p. 89.

19 Indeed, as Ciara Breathnach's recent book demonstrates, coroners' inquests can detail the ordinary person's life both inside and outside the home. Ciara Breathnach, *Ordinary Lives, Death, and Social Class: Dublin City Coroner's Court, 1876–1902* (Oxford: Oxford University Press, 2022).

20 For more information on professional and lay witnesses, see Vicky Holmes, 'Death of an Infant: Coroners' Inquests and the Study of Victorian Domestic Practice', *Home Cultures*, 11:3 (2014), 305–31. DOI: 10.2752/175174214X14035295691319.

21 Where the press was absent, such as in rural locations, some coroners would draft the press report to print. Holmes, 'Dangerous Spaces', pp. 71–3.

22 For more information on the preoccupation with death and coroners' inquests in the Victorian press, see L. Perry Curtis, *Jack the Ripper and the London Press* (New Haven, CT: Yale University Press, 2001); Holmes, 'Death of an Infant', 310–14; Michael MacDonald, 'Suicide and the Rise of the Popular Press in England', *Representations*, 22 (1988), 36–55.

23 Perry Curtis, *Jack the Ripper and the London Press*, p. 66.

24 The British Newspaper Archive contains a vast online repository of digitised British newspapers dating from the 1700s. www.britishnewspaperarchive.co.uk (accessed 5 February 2024).

1

The necessary lodger

Born in 1846, Mary Webb spent her childhood in the Oxfordshire hamlet of Burcot. Her parents, agricultural labourers, toiled in the fields to support their large family.[1] On reaching adulthood, Mary married Wiltshire-born labourer William Sloper. Briefly settling in Devizes, William's home town, Mary gave birth to their first son before they journeyed to Liverpool, where William took employment as a railway porter at Lime Street Station. The move, however, proved ill-fated.[2] In late 1881, William was crushed between the buffers of a goods train. Now a widow, the bereft Mary gathered her possessions and young children and returned to Oxfordshire, setting up a home at No. 6 Fisher Row in the centre of Oxford.[3] Mary 'worked hard … tak[ing] in washing and mangling' to support her family.[4] Yet Mary did not just take laundry into her home. At Fisher Row, Mary began taking in lodgers. Lodgers, like laundry, provided widows such as Mary an income without the need to go out to work. By May 1882, Mary had at least one lodger living under her roof, bricklayer John Wright, and around that same time, labourer Henry Burdock took lodgings in her home.[5] The following January, having 'knocked up an acquaintance', Henry married Mary.

There should have been little necessity for lodgers with a male breadwinner now in place, but this was not the case. Henry Burdock proved to be a drunk and violent husband and a poor provider, having 'no definite trade or occupation'.[6] As Mary's sister, Mercy Chesterman, informed newspaper reporters after Burdock's attempt on Mary's life, 'He has always been a loafer ever since I knew him he treated her very badly … When he was out of work, or in gaol, she kept the house going.'[7] Whether the Burdocks accommodated lodgers throughout their eight-and-a-half-year marriage is unclear. Certainly, by early 1887, the Burdocks, now residing at No. 5 Bridewell Square, were accommodating lodgers.[8] And by the summer of 1888, three lodgers were living under their roof: Mary's sister, her sister's husband, and a man named Dick Nicholls.[9] That same summer, following another gaol sentence for assaulting Mary and his dismissal from work, a violent row turned into a murderous attack. Conveyed to the hospital, Mary survived her husband's attempt on her life. Burdock, however, did not. He died by suicide.[10] After leaving the hospital, Mary maintained herself and her remaining dependent daughter through dressmaking and taking in lodgers.[11] Yet Mary's story does appear to have had somewhat of a silver lining, for in unmarried coachbuilder Henry Balkwell – who came to lodge under her roof sometime before the 1891 census – she found a more reliable breadwinner. Soon after Balkwell's arrival, the couple married, and from then on, I have found no record of lodgers in their home on Friar Street until after Henry died in 1912. In advancing years and with a daughter – described as an imbecile from childhood in the 1901 census – to support, Mary, now in her fifties, once again turned to accommodating lodgers.[12]

Mary's necessity for lodgers, both in bereavement and marriage, was not unique among the Victorian working class. Taking in lodgers was not, as is often perceived, solely the domain of female-headed households. Rather, as I will demonstrate, household income was supplemented or, in a few cases, entirely managed through accommodating lodgers in both male-headed and female-headed households as a consequence of both the inadequacies of the male breadwinner economy and the punitive nature of poor relief in this period. In the first part of this chapter, I examine the circumstances that drove the presence of lodgers in male-headed households, outlining that while 'bad' breadwinners such as Henry Burdock brought a dependence on lodgers, for many more, the lodger necessity was a result of low wages and financial instability brought on by unemployment, sickness, and physical decline. In the second part of this chapter, I look closely at the circumstance of the female-headed households compelled to accommodate lodgers, exploring their necessity for not just a lodger but rather multiple lodgers – alongside other labours – to make ends meet. Finally, while lodgers are generally perceived as the solution to financial difficulties for struggling households, I question whether taking in lodgers generated the income households so desperately sought.

Dominating the Victorian period was the breadwinner ideal, the idea that a husband provided solely for his family while his wife tended to the home and children. But as Sara Horrell and Jane Humphries, and more recently Emma Griffin, demonstrate, in reality, few working-class households could attain such an ideal. A working man's wage was often insufficient to maintain a family.[13] Across much of the family lifecycle, during underemployment or unemployment, accident or illness, or, as in the case of Mary Burdock, idleness, women and children's earnings augmented and, in some cases, even substituted for the male breadwinner wage. However, whereas children could go out to work, wives remained tied to the home in many areas of the country, supplementing their husbands' earnings through an economy of makeshifts, namely combining domestic labour such as charring, washing, and needlework alongside pawning, selling, or exchanging items when necessary.[14] Horrell and Humphries provide the example of a miner's wife who 'when times were hard in 1842, "[got] a little to make up the rent by making colliers' flannel shirts at 7d. apiece," paid for the black lead and mustard "by any little job" she could get, obtained salt in exchange for old bones, and took in a lodger!'[15] Crucial here is the presence of a lodger in the male-headed household. While husbands, as Humphries states, generally 'crowded out [the] option' of accommodating lodgers for income during the early industrial period,[16] when women found themselves increasingly aligned to the home, lodgers became an essential part of the economy of makeshifts. Indeed, Andrew Walker's investigation of the Victorian family wage in the colliery district of South Yorkshire identifies how lodgers were one of the few earnings available to miners' wives following the 1842 Mines and Collieries Act prohibiting women from working underground.[17] Yet as I demonstrate in this chapter, the necessity for a lodger in male-headed households was not limited to mining districts. Lodgers could be found across Victorian England in male-headed households, as was the case with widows and other female-headed households.

Lodgers also provided crucial income to Mary during her widowhoods, from young widowhood to old age. An untimely death frequently disrupted marriages in the Victorian period. As Michael Anderson's study of demographic change in England and Wales found, 19 per cent of couples marrying in the 1850s saw one spouse die within ten years, and more than 50 per cent within twenty-five years.[18] For working-class women, losing a husband was not just an emotional devastation but also a financial one. Few women could hope to recoup the equivalent of breadwinner wage. Immediate relief could be obtained at the workhouse doors, with many widows in the queue for outdoor relief during the first six months of their bereavement and possibly longer if there were dependent children to maintain.[19] Irrespective, however, the amount received would be far from sufficient to maintain a home and family. Instead, as Pat Thane outlines in her research on women and the New Poor Law, widowed mothers 'had always to find the means for supplementing [relief]'.[20] For these women, tied to the home, lodgers provided an expedient source of income. Indeed, as Jeff Meek has shown, some Poor Law authorities even began to actively encourage widows to take in lodgers, not only to ease the financial burden on the rate-payers but also 'to promote economic independence' and to ensure widows with children remained economically tied to the home.[21] Even on reaching old age, women – typically viewed as the 'deserving' poor – found themselves struggling with the bit of outrelief they got and could eventually, as will be seen, have few options beyond entering the workhouse.

Among Mary's neighbours, as she moved from street to street, there were likely to have been other female-headed households – those headed by married women – taking in lodgers in their struggle to make ends meet in the absence of their husbands, such as needlewoman Emma Prior, who lived at No. 29 Fisher Row on the night of the 1881 census.[22] We do not know what circumstances led Emma to be living without her husband. Imprisonment, emigration, military service, marital breakdown, or, quite simply, desertion placed many Victorian working-class women in the position of provider. Nonetheless, regardless of how their husbands departed, the wives left behind often had little, if any, means of financial support.[23] They had little hope of obtaining any support from the Poor Law guardians. As Thane explains, the guardians believed that providing outdoor relief to deserted families not only removed the responsibility of the husband/father but, they feared, it 'would encourage desertion by the husband, or even "collusion" between husband and wife in temporary desertion to gain relief for mothers and children in hard times'.[24] Similarly, few deserted working-class wives found remuneration through the courts. Even after the 1876 Act that empowered magistrates to order estranged husbands to provide for their wives and the Married Women's (Desertion) Act of 1886, which legally required it, many wives still did not receive the money granted to them under court order.[25] Unsurprisingly, then, deserted wives also turned to taking in lodgers, although these women, in particular, could not be choosey about the lodgers they took under their roof.

Male-headed households accommodating lodgers

Lodgers brought a share of the bread and butter to the table of male-headed working-class households across Victorian England. Indeed, in my sample of just under nine hundred inquest reports, almost half related to working-class households headed by married men with spouses present – 426 in total. Despite the perception of lodgers as the widow's domain, such numbers concur with the 1891 census (and prior censuses), with most lodgers and boarders enumerated on census night in Victorian England residing with married couples – 523,085 out of 853,638 households accommodating lodgers.[26] However, their reason for taking in a lodger varied widely across households, although nearly all had one thing in common: the failure of the male breadwinner economy.

Several cases in my sample identify working-class wives taking in lodgers to alleviate their financial troubles in the very trying circumstances experienced by Mary Burdock (née Webb, Sloper). For such women, whose husbands would not earn a living or simply spent what they had on drink, the financial burden of maintaining the family fell heavy upon their shoulders. Emma Griffin's examination of the Victorian breadwinner economy illustrates that families went hungry where husbands/fathers were too idle to work or 'drank away' their weekly wage packet.[27] In 1870s Birmingham, Charlotte Ball soon found herself in a straitened situation when she married a man of 'intemperate and idle habits'. Despite having an infant and another child not much older, Charlotte toiled as a brushmaker in a futile attempt to keep the family afloat. Falling into 'extreme poverty', to survive 'portions of the household furniture [were] sold on one or two occasions in order to provide them with proper food and clothing'. Seeking a more stable and regular income, Charlotte took in a lodger – an action that soon brought further discord to an already unhappy home. Believing his wife 'tended to show [a] marked preference for the lodger', John Ball, in an attempt to punish his wife for the unfounded misdemeanour, drowned his infant son in the Thames Valley canal.[28] There should have also been little necessity for lodgers in the Bradford home of recently wed twenty-five-year-old Mary Ann Johnson, whose husband was 'a clever hand at his trade and able to earn good wages'. Still, Mary Ann saw little of her husband's wage, for he spent much of what he earned 'indulg[ing] in … drunken orgies'. Unsurprisingly, their 'home [was] destitute of everything in the shape of comfort'. With a two-year-old child[29] and another on the way, Mary Ann took in 'one or more lodgers' to support them. Mary Ann's husband, however, affronted by the presence of lodgers in his home, jeopardised his wife's income through 'flatly and in course terms accus[ing] his wife of infidelity' with a male lodger and – in what today was a clear act of financial abuse – he threatened to 'sell all the furniture … and go "on the tramp."' It was a threat that drove Mary Ann to take her own life.[30]

Where a husband entirely refused to work or had simply drunk away all his wages, wives could become almost, if not wholly, dependent on the income from lodgers. With seven children and a 'great drunkard' for a husband, Ellen Holden found it necessary to squeeze four lodgers into her 'two-roomed' Sheffield home. However, while this may have alleviated some financial distress, it did little to improve her domestic situation: her lodgers also had far from temperate habits. Indeed, such was the drunken stupor they all returned in one Saturday night that it was only when one of the lodgers 'had sense enough left to ask for some tea' that they discovered Ellen was not asleep but dead on the hearth in front of them. At the inquest, the coroner, shocked by the evidence brought before him, stated, 'it was a disgrace that there should be such scenes in a place like Sheffield, where people earned good wages, and severely reprimanded the husband and lodger[s] for the way in which they had acted'.[31] Likewise, when fifteen-year-old Hannah Taylor married pig dealer James Taylor, a man twenty years her senior, he soon transpired to be a poor provider. Yet this was not a result of drunkenness eating the breadwinner wage but rather through 'indolent habits' not bringing in any wage.[32] Taylor simply refused to work. Instead, with their home in Tockenham conveniently placed near the Great Western Railway line, the Taylors 'principally relied for a maintenance upon taking in, as lodgers, some of the labourers on the railway'. Indeed, such was the reliance that the Taylors took in 'as many as ten' men into 'two little rooms', all of whom Hannah appeared to have prepared food for daily. As soon as she had finished with their breakfasts, she was immediately out in the garden, pulling and then preparing vegetables for the lodgers' dinner.[33]

Notably, the number of lodgers the Holdens and the Taylors accommodated would generally suggest the running of an established lodging house.[34] However, as the evidence of the inquest reports suggests, in some cases, a large number of lodgers in the home was not always a business venture but a mere matter of survival. Nevertheless, we must not assume that all those married couples who took in numerous lodgers had done so out of dire financial necessity. When thirty-eight-year-old Dorothy Clarke died in 1846, horseman Thomas Clarke – Dorothy's husband – informed the coroner that thirteen persons resided in their Kendal (Westmorland) home: themselves, their five children, and six lodgers. By all appearances, so many children alongside so many lodgers would signal a household struggling to keep their head above water. However, Dorothy's husband details her final meal, 'She had ham and eggs, and a little beef for supper.'[35] Such a protein-rich diet was a far cry from the diets of their peers, who survived on little more than bread when times were hard. Perhaps then, the Clarkes, as an exception rather than the norm, had taken in lodgers to improve their already reasonable standard of living.

Often, the lodger's time in these homes was fleeting, brought under the marital roof to alleviate immediate financial distress. Throughout the family lifecycle, working-class households were generally supported by the toil of the more temperate male breadwinner, albeit alongside the labours of their wives and children in an economy of makeshifts. Nonetheless, in various pinch points and crises, the lodger became a necessary part of such makeshifts. The arrival of children was one such pinch point. At least 200 of the 426 male-headed households accommodating lodgers in my sample – with both spouses present – had dependent children (those under eleven years). Lodgers appear to have, as Davidoff suggested, provided critical income when family size was at its most expansive and children were at their youngest.[36] Yet the lodger's presence was most prominent among those employed in low-wage or precarious occupations, whose wages were stretched to the absolute limits in housing, clothing, and feeding their expanding families.[37]

Some decades and distance apart, the following two cases parallel each other in their circumstances of two urban shoemakers struggling to maintain young and expanding families on their low and precarious incomes. Unable to resolve the family's poor circumstances, forty-six-year-old Henry John Battersbee was found drowned in the Regent Canal. Several London newspapers reporting on the 1846 coroner's inquest attributed, in their tagline, the cause of his death to be a result of 'SUICIDE INDUCED BY INCREASE OF FAMILY'. The reports detail how Battersbee struggled to maintain his growing family – his wife was recently confined with twins and six other children still at home – on his meagre earnings as a shoemaker. Therefore, they took in a lodger. Yet this did little to avail their straitened circumstances, for the lodger was unreliable in paying.[38] Even when a lodger was reliable in paying up each week, their contribution did not necessarily ease the financial burden upon the male breadwinner's wage. When thirty-eight-year-old Mary Sherwood died from a lack of nourishment and medical attention following a miscarriage in 1876, her husband, Nottingham shoemaker Alexander Sherwood, disclosed details to the coroner of his precarious earnings and his struggles to make ends meet: '[he] earned about 15s. a week … but last week he only earned about 10s. One of the children went out to work and got 2s. a week[,] and then there was 6s. 9d. rent to pay. The remaining money was all they had to live on' – 'they' being six children and his wife. An additional 2s. a week – one-third of the rent – came from taking in a female lodger, but even with this, Sherwood could not adequately feed his family or afford medical assistance for his wife.[39]

Notwithstanding the perception of lodgers as a predominantly urban phenomenon, some low-wage rural households in my sample also accommodated lodgers to compensate for the shortfall in the male breadwinner wage. Most of these – twenty-three in total – were agricultural or farm labourers who, like the shoemakers, found their wages falling short of maintaining a family. Despite being, as he described, in 'full work', agricultural labourer John Perry earned just '13s. a week wages', a wage far from sufficient to support a family of six. They had taken in a lodger to supplement his income, bringing an additional 2s. 6d. a week; but again, there was no buffer for emergencies. When his daughter was burnt as a result of an accident, Perry could not afford the medical treatment required, and a delay in receiving assistance brought about his daughter's untimely death.[40] Similarly, a solely occupied home was a far cry from what Derbyshire agricultural labourer William Robinson could afford for his family in his early marriage years. In August 1876, William's three-year-old son was mortally wounded after setting himself on fire with matches. Having extinguished the flames, his mother then left him with a lodger while she went for medical assistance.[41] As revealed in the 1871 census, with four young children aged seven and under to support on her husband's wages as an agricultural labourer, the Robinsons accommodated two lodgers, a married couple, in their home and well as 'huddling' with another family – a widow and her adult daughter.[42] Eventually, as they moved into a new phase of the lifecycle, the necessity for a lodger under their roof ceased. Indeed, the last recorded account of a lodger in their home was the above inquest. By the time of the 1881 census, the income from lodgers had been replaced by the wages of their two adolescent daughters in the silk mill.[43]

The wages of unmarried offspring might only create a decade or two reprieve for married couples having to accommodate lodgers to make ends meet. As the breadwinner wage decreased with age through what Matthew Woollard terms the process of 'deskilling', lodgers again became a necessary means of income for some ageing married couples.[44] In 1870s Nottingham, James Hummel struggled to maintain his trade as a framework knitter in increasing old age, turning instead to whatever unskilled labour he could obtain to support himself and his wife. After all, still being in some way 'able-bodied', he would, at this point of the Poor Law's story with the well-documented crusade against outdoor relief, unlikely have received any aid other than the workhouse. Unsurprisingly then, in his seventies, this once skilled worker was engaged in whitewashing, one of the most menial nineteenth-century labours. Yet despite having two employed (lace carders) unmarried adult daughters at home, Hummel's low and irregular wages meant that the family's combined earnings were still insufficient to sustain them. Therefore, they found it necessary to accommodate a lodger.[45] For some married couples, however, 'deskilling' was the first point at which they might have accommodated a lodger. Having never begotten children, the Leavers had lived relatively comfortably in their Oxford home. George Alexander Leaver had served 'Queen and Country' in India, from which he received a pension, and had, in his later years, obtained 'a very good place as a [constable] at the meat market'. Eventually, however, as George's health failed with age, the Leavers had to find other means to top up his army pension.[46] As the Victorian period drew into its final years, the Leavers decided on taking 'a larger house, seven shillings a week and the rates, thinking they might be better by having a lodger or two'.[47]

The lodger necessity, however, did not always follow the precise ebbs and flows of the working-class lifecycle. Crisis – at any point in the lifecycle – could also compel the temporary presence of a lodger in the home. In early industrial Britain, Humphries finds in her dataset (fifty-nine sources including contemporary social commentators, parliamentary papers, local archives, and village autobiographies) that 'no lodgers [were] present in the household of sick or unemployed men', arguing, as stated above, that 'a husband, even if ill and dependent, appears to have crowded out this option'.[48] Yet this is not the case in my sample of inquest reports.[49] I could simply argue Humphries's dataset merely missed those male-headed households accommodating lodgers. More likely, this situation occurred due to changes to outdoor relief coinciding approximately with the end of Humphries's data set – 1865 – and my sample's beginning – 1840. The New Poor Law of 1834 saw many Unions begin to dramatically reduce outdoor aid to adult males and was a move consolidated in the 1870s crusade against outdoor relief.[50] Therefore, for much of the Victorian period, when the breadwinner's wage was disrupted by unemployment, illness, or injury, many households abruptly faced destitution with little recourse to assistance beyond entering the workhouse, where families would become separated. The demand for cheap lodgings in many areas across England provided an immediate and often temporary respite for married couples living under the New Poor Law.

Seven such households in my sample reported the male head to be unemployed, while others stated that they had been unable to find employment in their trade and they had taken whatever labour they could find alongside the income from lodgers. For example, in 1864, John Hope informed Nottingham's coroner he was 'a collier by trade, but have not worked for some time'. In response to this information, the Coroner asked Hope, 'How do you obtain a livelihood?' he replied, 'I have gone rat-catching a bit.' With such little income, Hope resorted to taking in lodgers in his overcrowded two-roomed family home.[51] Surrey farm labourer William Brooker would have already struggled to maintain his household owing to his low wages, but when he fell ill in 1893 – 'laid up for nearly a year' – these wages ceased. His wife, Mary, did receive some outdoor relief to assist them and their two dependent children. Still, as was so often the case, such assistance was far from enough to sustain a household during a period of precarity.[52] Therefore, the Brookers temporarily took in a lodger to supplement the relief.[53] Similarly, in Newcastle-upon-Tyne in 1870, fifty-five-year-old Ann Walton found herself maintaining her children and husband, William, a labourer, who 'had not been working for some time, owing, it is said, to his having been in a rather low despondent condition of mind'. Like many women endeavouring to replace their husbands' lost wages, Ann earned her money through low-paid, home-based menial labour; she 'had a mangle and took in washing occasionally'. However, the household's only regular income came from their lodger.[54]

For some working-class households, the constant crisis of dire poverty led to the long-term accommodation of a lodger. The Vincents' married life was, it seems, one of permanent struggle. An inquest in Ipswich, 1894, revealed that Robert Vincent, a chemical works labourer, 'of late had done no work', and reports from the Police courts that same decade record the family as having stolen food out of hunger on at least two occasions. Their most consistent income appears to have come from their male lodger of fourteen years who, despite spending much of his wages on drink, was reliable in paying up each week. Nonetheless, despite the income from a lodger, Mrs Vincent was compelled to go 'out [to] work to keep herself and family from between eight and nine to six in the evening, with an hour for dinner'.[55]

Where working-class wives were faced with having to go out to work when their husbands could not, lodgers could serve a dual purpose in these households, for mothers, as Anderson has suggested, might leave their children under the care of a 'friendly lodger' when they had to work beyond the home.[56] With a regularly employed male lodger under her roof, we do not know who Mrs Vincent turned to care for her children while she was out at work. A female lodger was a much more practical solution for households where the mother routinely went out to work. With her husband also in the workhouse infirmary, Mrs Welch was left supporting her family on her 'scanty' earnings as a 'poor needlewoman'. She had refused to apply for relief, knowing all they would offer was the workhouse, and instead took a lodger into her Finsbury home.[57] Yet her reason for this was not just for additional income. A lodger also enabled her to continue to earn a living, for she would leave her one-year-old son 'with a lodger while she went out to work'.[58] Similarly, for Mrs Bull, of 22 Ruston Street, Parnell Road, London, her husband's ailing health made 'it necessary for [her] to go out to work in order to keep the home together', and she left her children in the care of a lodger whilst her eldest child was at school.[59]

Notably, while many husbands would have conceded to the necessity of such an arrangement, some were evidently scornful of this role reversal. In London in 1879, Jane Cordelia Burgess married bicycle maker Thomas Jukes, and in the decade that followed, they had at least four children. The 1891 census portrays Thomas as the family's sole earner, and he may have been at the time.[60] However, the family's circumstances changed shortly after that, and a lodger became a critical part of their story. Investigating the death of the couple's eldest daughter in March 1894, thirteen-year-old Hester, the coroner's court found that Jane's own husband had reported her to the *Society for the Prevention of Cruelty to Children* for neglecting their children. His complaint was that she 'went out to work without his consent'. Pressed further by the coroner, the husband's negligence claim began to unravel as he revealed 'he had been out of work since August last, and that his wife had during that time supported the family ... work[ing] as a cook'. Yet it was not he who cared for their children in her absence. This task fell to the household's lodger, Mrs Westropp. As Mrs Westropp confirmed, 'she looked after Mrs Jukes children, whilst she went *out* to work'. Perhaps unsurprising, the coroner found no evidence of the charges made by the husband and instead 'commended [Mrs Jukes] for the effort on behalf of the children'.[61] In other cases, the lodger became part of the wider economy when wives were compelled to financially and domestically maintain the family home. With five children under twelve years old and a husband in the Limehouse workhouse infirmary, Sarah Page became increasingly dependent on her lodger, fifty-nine-year-old Susannah Dunmore, to keep the rest of them out of the workhouse – the Poor Law guardians having refused outrelief. But this was not through direct payment of lodgings. Instead, Page and Dunmore worked together 'slop stitching … mak[ing] a shilling a day'.[62]

Of course, some male-headed households that were headed by lone men – either married men whose spouses were absent or widowers – also accommodated lodgers.[63] They are infrequent, accounting for only twenty-eight households in my sample.[64] The one thing that ties these men together is that the lodgers had tended to be present in their homes before the marital breakdown or bereavement. 'Living apart' from his wife, fifty-two-year-old Islington dairyman Richard Harvey had remained in the marital home, 'the house [being] attached to his place of business'. He did not, however, reside alone. While Harvey lived in the front parlour, the rest of his home was occupied by lodgers already resident before the couple's separation.[65] But given the level of service often required in these domestic dwelling lodging arrangements – as discussed in detail in Chapter 3 – there is the overarching question as to how these lone men managed both their homes and lodgers and, as Lenore Davidoff asked in the case of such men, 'Who does for him?'[66] In some cases, this role fell to the female lodger. For example, following his wife's death, his daughters leaving home, and his complete withdrawal from employment, the ageing James Hummel, whom we have already met, continued to keep lodgers. But this decision was not just a financial one. Despite his decrepitude, Hummel managed to 'provide himself with his own food', but he relied on his female lodger, Mary Jones, to keep house. As Jones informed the coroner's court investigating Hummel's death, 'she undertook the cleaning of the house'.[67] Similarly, in 1880s London, Robert Gardener and his family lodged with a widower who lived alone and, as part of their arrangement, his 'wife used to clean his rooms and make his bed for him'.[68]

Female-headed households accommodating lodgers

Absent male breadwinners – either through abandonment, separation, or death – also necessitated the presence of a lodger or, in
most cases, lodgers, in the home. At least 190 female heads were
determined in my sample of households takings in lodgers, but it
is likely that more female heads were hidden behind the cases of
undetermined household status (249), where many refer to a nameless woman or only refer to them as 'Mrs' followed by the surname,
leaving actual marital status ambiguous and difficult to trace in
other documentary evidence. Of those marital statuses determined,
twenty-five female heads were married, 136 were widows, and just
twenty-nine were spinsters.[69] For those women with absent but still
living husbands, there was – as noted above – little recourse for
financial assistance. For many of these women, daily survival came
in the form of a lodger. Louisa Ferris maintained herself by accommodating lodgers, albeit with some help, after a marital breakdown.
Having married carrier William Ferris 'at the early age of sixteen',
she experienced physical abuse throughout their short-lived marriage.[70] Just over a decade later, in 1845, the marriage entirely broke
down. With no financial support forthcoming from her estranged
husband, Louisa turned to her parents. Her 'mother and stepfather
[having] consulted as to the best means of supporting her … took
and furnished [a] house in Lion Street, Bristol, under the idea that,
by taking in lodgers, she might half contribute to the support of herself and her children', rather than become a burden upon them. A
year later, Louisa had four lodgers living under her roof, including a
man who – while known to her – was, as I will return to in Chapter
5, a less than desirable lodger.[71]

In the case of marital separation, the necessity for a lodger often
left these women little choice as to who to take in as lodgers, as
exemplified at a coroner's inquest held in Norwich in 1858. Called
to testify regarding the death of an illegitimate infant under her
roof, Maria Ann Melton informed the court that her husband,
Henry, a butcher, had, as far as she was aware, left for Australia six
years previously – a route that allowed him to escape any responsibility for her maintenance. Maria Ann then had to find the means
to keep the roof over her head.[72] For Maria Ann, this was taking
in any lodger – including a soon-to-be confined single woman,

Maria Pleasance – that would help to pay the rent. As discussed in Chapter 2, unmarried mothers could find themselves turned away from potential lodgings and, therefore, often presented themselves as married women to obtain them. Still, Melton did not turn away Pleasance, despite being aware of her lodger's situation, for she needed the income:[73] 'I did not know her before. I knew she was in the family way ... I took her in because I could not pay my rent without a lodger.' But as her lodger paid her just 18d. (1s. 6d.) a week, this amount would have hardly covered Maria Ann's rent, let alone her everyday living expenses.[74] Like many other women in her position, Melton probably sustained herself through a number of other makeshift labours alongside the income from lodgers.

While lodgers were a significant recourse for female-headed households, even when multiple lodgers were accommodated, the income from taking in lodgers was generally insufficient to parallel the earnings of a male breadwinner. Therefore, alongside the domestic burden associated with accommodating lodgers, these women were also forced to seek some form of employment. Generally, these women sought domestic employment, being more compatible with seeing to children and lodgers. For example, following marital breakdown, thirty-three-year-old Mary Miller had to support herself and her daughter. Though we do not have an account of all the years between separating from her husband and her murder around ten years later, we know that she resided at No. 6, St. Mary's Place, Moston, Manchester, for the final three years of her life. Here, appearing to have no financial assistance from her estranged husband, 'she earned her living by dressmaking and letting lodgings, her lodgers for the most part being females', removing the domestic burden that came with accommodating male lodgers. As will be discussed in Chapter 3, female lodgers were generally expected to see to themselves. However, when necessary, Mary also accommodated male lodgers.[75] While not legally married, Annie Burnett lived with a man with whom she had at least one child, and when he emigrated to Australia, she also had to find the means to support her family. As an unmarried mother, Annie was unlikely to receive any form of poor relief except for the workhouse. Instead, as an experienced domestic servant, she did 'a good deal of charing' and took lodgers into her small home.[76] Despite the daily toil of work, keeping lodgings, and caring for her children, Annie still managed to provide a clean and comfortable home. The shared living space was described at a coroner's inquest as:

> particularly clean in appearance ... In the centre of the floor stood a table, spotlessly white with continued scouring and washing. Various framed coloured plates and photographs adorned the walls, while the furniture consisting of a couple of chairs and a settee, along with the window curtains, showed that no small amount of pains had been taken to make everything as comfortable as possible for a woman with a small means to make a home.[77]

Not all married women with absent husbands turned to domestic occupations alongside lodgers. Having married Albert Rayner, a Cambridgeshire baker, in 1890, by 1897, Emma Julia Rayner, now with three children, found herself deserted by her husband. While he initially maintained the family he left behind, the financial support soon ceased. Despite attempts to obtain the money owed in maintenance through the courts, she was left entirely unsupported. Yet by some means, Emma established her own business. Moving to the centre of Cambridge, Emma hired a small sweet-stuff shop and took in two male lodgers 'in her endeavour to maintain herself and children'. However, while she appeared to have been relatively successful at this venture, as inquest witnesses testified, she was so troubled by the breakdown of her marriage that, eventually, Emma murdered her children before taking her own life.[78]

Death, like desertion, left women scrambling to keep the roof over their heads. While some with children might have found temporary alleviation through outdoor relief, in their respectable status as widows, that given was rarely sufficient to meet the bare minimal requirements for living. Therefore, in their grief, widows were immediately tasked with finding the means to support themselves and any dependents. The Halifax coroner's inquest investigating the death of forty-five-year-old Martha Stephenson exemplifies just how quickly these women had to act after losing their husbands. Just nineteen weeks before her own death, Martha's husband – a wool wholesale bookkeeper – had died unexpectedly, leaving her 'in but poor circumstances' and Martha, since his death, 'obtain[ed] her livelihood by keeping lodgers' – something she does not appear to have done at any previous point.[79]

Yet as hinted at by the plural 'lodgers', widows typically had to accommodate more than one lodger to reconstitute a similar level of male breadwinner earnings, as Betty Scott soon also found. Having married carter William Scott in 1868 in her home parish of Habergham Eaves, Burnley, Betty was expecting their fourth child by the time of his death from pneumonia in 1876.[80] Considered in the community to be a woman who 'kept herself and her children respectable', the guardians granted her application for outdoor relief. However, the relief was insufficient to sustain the family long term.[81] Betty, therefore, took in washing and a female lodger (as a boarder), but, as Humphries identifies in the case of female-headed households, Betty was also somewhat dependent on her children's earnings. Indeed, the Poor Law Guardian themselves might have encouraged it, for both of Betty's sons – aged about eleven and ten years respectively – were, by 1871, it appears, employed at the local print works.[82] The death of Betty's eldest son, James, from typhoid fever and the loss of his wages that same year seems to be the catalyst for the arrival of further lodgers into her home, for shortly after, Robert Gilfillan, Edward Carling, and Robert Templeton, all machine printers at the print works also employing Betty's sons, took up lodgings in her home. Betty's daily domestic toil must have been relentless. As the *Burnley Express* noted when reporting on her death, 'She fought bravely to keep herself and her family [including a dependent brother] and was generally considered one of the most industrious, clean, and laborious women in the place.'[83]

Ageing widows also maintained themselves by taking in lodgers alongside other labours. For example, in the 1880s, following the death of her husband, wool-sorter Richard Ashfield, Amelia Ashfield, in her seventies, let part of her Oxford home to lodgers, 'two workmen'. Yet she did not entirely depend on the income from lodgers, for the census records her occupation as 'needlewoman'.[84] When Alice Brimelow lost her husband and a wage-earning son, she, in her mid-fifties, commenced employment alongside her adult stepchildren at Tyldesley cotton mill. Nonetheless, her wages would have fallen short of those lost, prompting Alice to take lodgers into her home. Indeed, this proved a reliable source of income for Alice. One of her lodgers – unmarried cotton mill labourer John Hampson – arrived shortly after her husband's death and remained at least for the next seventeen years, as he informed Tyldesley's coroner.[85]

In some cases, despite their advanced age, these widows had to find various means of supplementing their income because they still had dependents to support. As noted earlier, Mary Sloper, following the death of her third husband, returned to accommodating lodgers to support herself and her dependent daughter. In the case of Hull resident Elizabeth McKay, a widow in her fifties with two children – one of whom did 'maintain herself', the other being still dependent – the inquest report records her total income from lodgers and other means: 'Three lodgers who pay one shilling and sixpence a week each' and going out to work two or three days a week, all added to an income of around 8s. a week. If her rent were that of the neighbouring house, McKay would have had just under 7s. a week for food and other necessities.[86]

In some cases, widows clubbed together to keep the roof over their heads. Frances Hatfield and Caroline Marks had lived cheek-by-jowl in George Yard, St Giles – one of London's notorious slums – for more than thirty years. During this time, both had been wed and widowed. Impoverished both in marriage and bereavement, Caroline and Frances toiled away in their neighbouring homes. Caroline made around 4s. a week selling hooks to butchers, and Hatfield – with a brother recently discharged from Colney asylum under her roof to care for – earned just 1s. 6d. a week cleaning pots for publicans. Yet such amounts were insufficient to make the weekly rent on their single-roomed homes. The solution for Frances was to have 'the shilling a week rent she paid … allowed her by a lodger, whom she took into her room'. That lodger was Caroline.[87]

Conclusion

The lodger necessity was borne out of the breadwinner ideology that had firmly taken hold by the Victorian era, pushing women out of the traditional labour force and shaping the punitive administration of the New Poor Law. Yet as widely observed, dependence on the male breadwinner wage shaped by ideals did not work in reality. Low wages, underemployment, unemployment, sickness or – at worst – idleness and drunkenness on the part of the male breadwinner brought working-class households to the brink of destitution, leaving wives and children to make up the deficit. I have demonstrated in this chapter that alongside a range of widely acknowledged makeshift and meagre employment economies, the lodger appears to have played a more prominent role than has generally been thought in the male-headed working-class home when it came to making ends meet. However, as will be explored in Chapter 4, with such households generally only having space for one or two lodgers at the most, they only went a little way to alleviate the family's economic distress.

The failure of the breadwinner model also fed into the financial straits of female-headed households and their necessity to accommodate lodgers. As I have demonstrated in this chapter, the refusal of the Poor Law authorities to support wives in the absence of the husband and the pittance widows received in the form of outdoor relief placed the burden of survival squarely on her shoulders. Therefore, while male-headed households typically took in just one lodger to ease financial difficulties, female-headed households – in the struggle to come anywhere near to replicating the male wage – were compelled to take multiple lodgers alongside other domestic labours to keep the roof over their heads. With their days filled with backbreaking domestic toil and attending to several working men, it is little surprise then that Mary Sloper married two of her lodgers, hoping, perhaps, to ease the domestic drudgery. Yet lodgers – despite their prevalence – only provided a safety net when they could be retained. Lodgers, as will be explored in the following chapters, were not necessarily the panacea we have come to assume for female-headed households. Nonetheless, they were still a critical part of their story, as I will continue to demonstrate throughout the book. But now we have met those in Victorian working-class England who accommodated lodgers, we turn to the next chapter to meet the lodgers themselves and understand the circumstances that brought about the lodging necessity.

Notes

1 The occupations of both Mary's father, Joseph, and mother, Ann, are recorded in the 1851 and 1861 census as 'agricultural labourer'. The National Archives (TNA), HO107/1847, f. 569, p. 23, s. 12, 1851 England, Wales & Scotland Census; TNA, RG09/734, f. 6, p. 6,

1861 England, Wales & Scotland Census via www.findmypast.co.uk (accessed 5 February 2024).

2 TNA, RG10/1914, f. 58, p. 10, s. 46, 1871 England, Wales & Scotland Census; TNA, RG11/3702, f. 112, p. 4, s. 911, 1881 England, Wales & Scotland Census.

3 *Jackson's Oxford Journal*, 13 May 1882, p. 8; *Oxfordshire Weekly News*, 15 August 1888, p. 2.

4 Moring, *Female Economic Strategies*, p. 59. For information on the range of paid work undertaken in female-headed households, see Jane Humphries, 'Female-Headed Households in Early Industrial Britain: The Vanguard of the Proletariat?', *Labour History Review*, 63:1 (1998), 31–65. DOI: 10.3828/lhr.63.1.31.

5 We know of Wright's presence as a lodger in No. 6 Fisher Row because he was summoned and charged by Oxford City Police Court for stealing from Mary – a sovereign and two coins on a chain – for which he served one month's hard labour. *Jackson's Oxford Journal*, 13 May 1882, p. 8.

6 Various newspaper reports detail Burdock's violent behaviour, surmised in an 1888 report by the *Oxfordshire Weekly News*: 'all neighbours testify to the fact that quarrels between [Burdock] and his wife were almost a daily occurrence, which is attested by the police records. On the 4th of December, 1883, Burdock was bound over to keep the peace towards his wife for six months. On June 10th, 1884, he was fined 2s. 6d., and 3s. 6d. costs, and bound over himself in £5 to keep the peace for six months for a similar offence. On September 16th, 1887, he was again summoned for assaulting her and fined 1s., and 3s. cost, and bound over as before. On the 21st of October 1887, husband and wife took out cross-summonses against each other, and both were bound over to keep the peace. Finally, on 29th June last, Burdock was sentenced to a month's imprisonment for violently assaulting his wife.' *Oxfordshire Weekly News*, 15 August 1888, p. 2.

7 *Oxfordshire Weekly News*, 15 August 1888, p. 2.

8 The first reference of a lodger at this address was Joseph Webb, brother-in-law to the Burdocks, charged with assaulting Henry. *Jackson's Oxford Journal*, 26 March 1887, p. 5.

9 *Jackson's Oxford Journal*, 18 August 1888, p. 6.

10 *Oxfordshire Weekly News*, 15 August 1888, p. 2.

11 On the night of the census of 1891, an unmarried coachbuilder, Henry Balkwell, and an unmarried baker, Walter Betteriss, were residing – as lodgers – under Mary's roof. TNA, RG12/1167, f. 38, p. 25, s. 162, 1891 England, Wales & Scotland Census.

12 This is found in reference to Mary's son Joseph being charged on a warrant with using threatening language to his mother. One of the key witnesses was James Henry Atkins, a lodger. *Oxford Chronicle and Reading Gazette*, 15 August 1913, p. 11.

13 As Sara Horrell and Jane Humphries found in their research on the origins and expansion of the male breadwinner family in mid-nineteenth-century Britain, 'apart from factory workers, in the early nineteenth century, men were not able to earn a family wage in a sense of being able to increase their earnings in line with the demands of a growing family. Instead, it was women's and children's earnings which augmented incomes in the face of additional needs as family size and the age of children rose.' Sara Horrell and Jane Humphries, 'The Origins and Expansion of the Male Breadwinner Family: The Case of Nineteenth-Century Britain', *International Review of Social History*, 42:s5 (1997), 38. DOI: 10.1017/S0020859000114786. See also Sara Horrell and Jane Humphries, '"The Exploitation of Little Children": Child Labor and the Family Economy in the Industrial Revolution', *Explorations in Economic History*, 32:4 (1995), 485–516. DOI: 10.1006/exeh.1995.1021; Emma Griffin, 'Diets, Hunger and Living Standards During the British Industrial Revolution', *Past & Present*, 239:1 (2018), 71–111. DOI: 10.1093/pastj/gtx061; Emma Griffin, *Bread Winner: An Intimate History of the Industrial Revolution* (New Haven, CT: Yale University Press, 2020). For a long view, see Sara Horrell, Jane Humphries, and Jacob Weisdorf, 'Beyond the Male Breadwinner: Life-Cycle Living Standards of Intact and Disrupted English Working Families, 1260–1850', *Economic History Review*, 75:2 (2022), 530–60. DOI: 10.1111/ehr.13105.

14 See above note; also see Samantha Williams, 'Earnings, Poor Relief and the Economy of Makeshifts: Bedfordshire in the Early Years of the New Poor Law', *Rural History*, 16:1 (2005), 21–52. DOI: 10.1017/S0956793304001293. For more information on pawning, selling, and exchanging, see Ellen Ross, 'Survival Networks: Women's Neighbourhood Sharing in London before World War 1', *History Workshop*, 15 (1983), 4–27; Melanie Tebbutt, *Making Ends Meet: Pawnbroking and Working-Class Credit* (Leicester: Leicester University Press, 1983).

15 Sara Horrell and Jane Humphries, 'Women's Labour Force Participation and the Transition to the Male-Breadwinner Family, 1790–1865', *The Economic History Review*, 48:1 (1995), 98–9. DOI: 10.2307/2597872.

16 Humphries, 'Female-Headed Households', 39.

17 Andrew Walker, 'Pleasurable Homes? Victorian Model Miners' Wives and the Family Wage in a South Yorkshire Colliery District', *Women's History Review*, 6:3 (1997), 317–36. DOI: 10.1080/09612029700200147.
Humphries and Thomas' recent work on household labour also discussed the presence of the lodger in the miner's home concerning the additional labour this resulted in for the women of the of the house. Jane Humphries and Ryah Thomas (2023), '"The Best Job in the World": Breadwinning and the Capture of Household Labor in Nineteenth and Early Twentieth-Century British Coalmining', *Feminist Economics*, 29:1 (2023), 97–140. DOI: 10.1080/13545701.2022.2128198

18 Michael Anderson, 'The Social Implications of Demographic Change', in F. M. L. Thompson (ed.), *The Cambridge Social History of Britain*, Vol. 2 (Cambridge: Cambridge University Press, 1990), pp. 29–30.

19 Julie-Marie Strange, *Death, Grief and Poverty in Britain, 1870–1914* (Cambridge: Cambridge University Press, 2010), pp. 196–200. Widows were granted outdoor relief for the first six months 'and for an indeterminate time if they had dependent children'. Relief stopped, however, if the widow bore an illegitimate child. Lynn Hollen Lees, *The Solidarities of Strangers: The English Poor Laws and the People, 1700–1948* (Cambridge: Cambridge University Press, 2006), p. 201.

20 Pat Thane, 'Women and the Poor Law in Victorian and Edwardian England', *History Workshop*, 6 (1978), 41.

21 Jeff Meek, 'Boarding and Lodging Practices in Early Twentieth-Century Scotland', *Continuity and Change*, 31:1 (2016), 79–100, 92–3. DOI: 10.1017/S0268416016000084.

22 TNA, RG11/1503, f. 110, p. 7, s. 941, 1881 England, Wales & Scotland Census.

23 For more information on the circumstances of marital separation and desertion among the Victorian working class, see Griffin, *Bread Winner*, pp. 135–59; Vicky Holmes, *In Bed with the Victorians: The Life-Cycle of Working-Class Marriage* (Cham: Palgrave Macmillan, 2017), pp. 65–82; Humphries, 'Female-Headed Households', 33–4; Marjorie Levine-Clark, 'From "Relief" to "Justice and Protection": The Maintenance of Deserted Wives, British Masculinity, and Imperial Citizenship, 1870–1920', *Gender and History*, 22:2 (2010), 302–21. DOI: 10.1111/j.1468-0424.2010.01592.x; Lesley Trotter, *The Married Widows of Cornwall: The Story of the Wives 'Left Behind' by Emigration* (Cheltenham: Humble History Press, 2018).

24 Thane, 'Women and the Poor Law', 37.

25 Even after the 1876 Act that empowered magistrates to order estranged husbands to provide for their wives and the Married Women's (Desertion) Act of 1886, which legally required it, many wives still did

not receive the money granted to them under court order. For more information, see Levine-Clark, 'The Maintenance of Deserted Wives', 302–3; Thane, 'Women and the Poor Law', 29–51.

26 Kevin Schürer and Edward Higgs, Integrated Census Microdata (I-CeM), 1851–1911. [data collection]. UK Data Service. SN: 7481 (2020). DOI: 10.5255/UKDA-SN-7481-2. 1881 census: 575,940 out of 884,811; 1861 census: 443,068 out of 648,090; 1851 census: 312,799 out of 479,649.

27 As Emma Griffin concludes, 'The single greatest cause of hunger, however, was drunkenness: seven autobiographies reported that their own or their father's drinking had left them (or their families) without food to eat', Emma Griffin, 'Diets, Hunger and Living Standards during the British Industrial Revolution', *Past & Present*, 239:1 (2018), 71–111. DOI: 10.1093/pastj/gtx061. For other examples, see Griffin, *Bread Winner*, pp. 117–19, 124, 202, 231–2.

28 Confessing immediately after the act, he spent the rest of his days in Broadmoor, dying in 1903 at the age of fifty. I have yet to uncover what became of Charlotte following this tragic event. *Birmingham Mail*, 26 June 1876, p. 3; *Birmingham & Aston Chronicle*, 1 July 1876, p. 5; *Aris's Birmingham Gazette*, 14 October 1876, p. 6; *Leamington Spa Courier*, 9 December 1876, p. 7; *Birmingham Daily Post*, 9 January 1877, p. 6.

29 Their first child had been born out of wedlock, presumably because they did not have the means to marry, as could often be the case amongst the poorest in society at this time. John R. Gillis, *For Better, For Worse: British Marriages, 1600 to the Present* (New York: Oxford University Press, 1985), pp. 231–59.

30 *Bradford Observer*, 30 December 1852, p. 5; *Leeds Times*, 1 January 1853, p. 5.

31 *Sheffield Daily Telegraph*, 1 February 1870, p. 8.

32 One report suggests her having previously cohabited with Hannah's widowed mother! *Royal Cornwall Gazette*, 17 July 1840, p. 2.

33 *Devizes and Wiltshire Gazette*, 9 July 1840, p. 3. He was sentenced to death, *Devizes and Wiltshire Gazette*, 18 March 1841, p. 3.

34 Michael Anderson, *Family Structure in Nineteenth-Century Lancashire* (Cambridge: Cambridge University Press, 1971), p. 47.

35 *Kendal Mercury*, 4 April 1846, p. 3.

36 Leonore Davidoff, 'The Separation of Home and Work? Landladies and Lodgers in Nineteenth- and Twentieth-Century England', in Sandra Burman (ed.), *Fit Work for Women* (London: Croom Helm, 1979), pp. 64–97, 83–4.

37 There is perhaps some regional variation in those who took in lodgers at this point in the lifecycle. Andrew Walker noted in his study of South Yorkshire's colliery district that the poorest homes did not have room to accommodate a lodger. Walker, 'Pleasurable Homes', 327–30.

38 It is likely that his older children, Henry, William, George, and perhaps even ten-year-old Frederick, would have been contributing to the household purse, but their meagre wages were evidently not enough. *Sun* (London), 6 November 1846, p. 4; *Morning Post*, 5 November 1846, p. 6.

39 *Nottingham Journal*, 29 February 1876, p. 3.

40 The incumbent, in response to Perry's plight, granted 'him a note to the relieving officer' at Walsall. However, a miscommunication at Walsall meant that Perry's daughter never received medical assistance, and she died from her injuries. The medical witness at the inquest stated that 'in all human probability the child's life would have been saved' had medical aid been called upon. *Birmingham Daily Post*, 23 March 1858, p. 2; *Birmingham Journal*, 27 March 1858, p. 7.

41 *Sheffield Daily Telegraph*, 25 August 1876, p. 4.

42 TNA, RG10/3561, f. 37, p. 17 s. 79, 1871 England, Wales & Scotland Census.

43 TNA, RG11/3405, f. 79, p. 19 s. 624, 1881 England, Wales & Scotland Census.

44 For more information on the process of deskilling, see Matthew Woollard, 'The Employment and Retirement of Older Men, 1851–1881: Further Evidence from the Census', *Continuity and Change*, 17 (2002), 437–63. DOI: 10.1017/S0268416002004381

45 TNA, HO107/8676, f. 31, p. 17, s. 682, 1841 England, Wales & Scotland Census; TNA, RG09/2459, f. 123, p. 39, s. 206, 1861 England, Wales & Scotland Census; TNA, RG10/3517, f. 64, p. 5, s. 27, 1871 England, Wales & Scotland Census; *Nottingham Journal*, 30 October 1876, p. 3; *Nottinghamshire Guardian*, 3 November 1876, p. 5.

46 The inquest report pertaining to the death of sixty-one-year-old George Alexander Leaver stated that he had occupied this position for nineteen years but four years prior had to leave employment on suffering from a diseased liver. *Oxfordshire Weekly News*, 10 December 1890, p. 6.

47 *Oxford Times*, 11 August 1900, p. 7; *Oxford Times*, 18 August 1900, p. 5.

48 Humphries, 'Female-Headed Households', 39.

49 Similarly, in her examination of lodging in the late nineteenth and early twentieth centuries, Beatrice Moring found that 'In poor families with unemployed or disabled heads, keeping three or four lodgers could be a way of making ends meet.' Beatrice Moring, 'Introduction: Lodgers

in Rural and Urban Europe in the Past', *Continuity and Change*, 31:1 (2016), 5. DOI: 10.1017/S0268416016000072.

50 Hollen Lees, *The Solidarities of Strangers*, pp. 210–17.

51 *Nottingham Journal*, 6 April 1864, p. 3.

52 Hollen Lees, *The Solidarities of Strangers*, p. 201.

53 *Sussex Agricultural Express*, 23 January 1894, p. 3.

54 *Bradford Daily Telegraph*, 8 March 1870, p. 4; *Newcastle Courant*, 11 March 1870, p. 2.

55 TNA, RG12/1468, f. 127, p. 5, s. 27, 1891 England, Wales & Scotland Census; *Ipswich Journal*, 6 January 1894, p. 2. In 1892, Vincent's eleven-year-old son was charged with stealing '4 lbs of maize, value 6d'. In his defence, 'The boy said his father had been out of work all week and had only earned one shilling.' Being his first offence – and hearing from Maria on the family poverty – the magistrate dismissed the case. Following Last's death in 1894, the family's struggles continued. In 1898, desperate to abate his family's hunger, Robert Vincent stole two dead fowls, valued at 5s. *East Anglian Daily Times*, 14 October 1892, p. 3; *East Anglian Daily Times*, 18 October 1892, p. 3; (Ipswich) *Evening Star*, 9 May 1898, p. 2.

56 Anderson, *Family Structure*, p. 74.

57 For more information on the refusal to apply for relief, see Vicky Holmes, 'Pulling Back the Covers: Uncovering Beds in the Victorian Working-Class Home', in Joseph Harley, Vicky Holmes, and Laika Nevalainen (eds), *The Working Class at Home, 1790–1940* (Cham: Palgrave Macmillan, 2022), pp. 73–95.

58 *London Evening Standard*, 22 October 1864, p. 5. The mother is not directly named in the inquest report.

59 *Reynold's Newspaper*, 21 May 1882, p. 8. She, too, was not named directly in the inquest report.

60 TNA, RG12/42, f. 18, p. 39 s. 285, 1891 England, Wales & Scotland Census.

61 Emphasis author's own. Hester, it was concluded, had died from blood poisoning, resulting from an injury from a vice falling upon her knee. The coroner's jury returned a verdict of accidental death. *Kilburn Times*, 17 March 1894, p. 3.

62 Sarah Page also informed the coroner's court that she had herself only recently left the (Bromley) workhouse infirmary. Dunmore then informed the coroner's court that during Sarah's stay in the workhouse infirmary in consequence of a fever, 'the workhouse people gave them four loaves a week, but no meat or moneys'. And in February 1864, a coroner's inquest determined that the Pages' youngest child,

three-year-old Ellen, had died 'from exposure to cold, and from want of food and proper clothing'. *Lloyd's Weekly Newspaper*, 21 February 1864, p. 3.

63 The one recorded bachelor taking in lodgers in my search appears to have been 'letting rooms', suggesting he was running in the style of a lodging house rather than accommodating lodgers in 'his home'.

64 As the I-CeM reveals, on the night of the 1891 census in England, male-headed households – widowed, married spouse absent – made up just 32,597 of the householders accommodating lodgers and boarders in private dwellings. Kevin Schürer and Edward Higgs, Integrated Census Microdata (I-CeM), 1851–1911. [data collection]. UK Data Service. SN: 7481 (2020). DOI: 10.5255/UKDA-SN-7481-2.

65 *North London News*, 2 January 1864, p. 5.

66 Leonore Davidoff, *Worlds Between: Historical Perspectives on Gender and Class* (Cambridge: Polity Press, 1995), p. 161.

67 *Nottingham Journal*, 30 October 1876, p. 3; *Nottinghamshire Guardian*, 3 November 1876, p. 5.

68 *The People*, 21 May 1882, p. 9.

69 In England, on the night of the 1891 census, 167,239 widows, 45,670 single, 29,792 married spouse absent, 10 divorced, were accommodating lodgers and boarders. Kevin Schürer and Edward Higgs, Integrated Census Microdata (I-CeM), 1851–1911. [data collection]. UK Data Service. SN: 7481 (2020). DOI: 10.5255/UKDA-SN-7481-2.

70 Newspaper reports prior to their separation reveal that William was a violent and abusive husband. *Bristol Times and Mirror*, 15 February 1845, p. 2.

71 *Bristol Mercury*, 7 November 1846, p. 2; *Bristol Times and Mirror*, 7 November 1846, p. 1.

72 It is possible that, from at least 1861 onward, Henry was living in Colton (next to East Tuddenham, Norwich) where a man of the same name was listed as a butcher in the census. In 1855, he had married the woman with whom he was resident on the night of the census, so it is possible that Maria Ann had not been legally married to Henry. There is a record of a Henry Melton marrying Mary Ann in 1849, citing potential bigamy. TNA, RG09/1221, f. 55, p. 2, s. 8, 1861 England, Wales & Scotland Census. For further discussion on the issues of emigration and the maintenance of the wives left behind, see Levine-Clark, 'The Maintenance of Deserted Wives', 302–21.

73 Samantha K. Williams, '"I Was Forced to Leave My Place to Hide My Shame": The Living Arrangements of Unmarried Mothers in London in the Early Nineteenth Century', in Joanne McEwan and Pamela Sharpe (eds), *Accommodating Poverty: The Housing and Living Arrangements*

of the English Poor, c.1600–1850 (Basingstoke: Palgrave Macmillan, 2010), p. 204. See also Vicky Holmes, 'Accommodating the Lodger: The Domestic Arrangements of Lodgers in Working-Class Dwellings in a Victorian Provincial Town', *Journal of Victorian Culture*, 19:3 (2014), 324–26. DOI: 10.1080/13555502.2014.947181.

74 *Norfolk Chronicle*, 18 December 1858, p. 6; *Norwich Mercury*, 18 December 1858, p. 6.

75 *Manchester Courier and Lancashire General Advertiser*, 2 March 1888, p. 8; *Manchester Courier and Lancashire General Advertiser*, 1 March 1888, p. 8.

76 *Yorkshire Post and Leeds Intelligencer*, 8 November 1894, p. 6.

77 *Daily Gazette for Middlesbrough*, 8 November 1894, p. 3; *Daily Gazette for Middlesbrough*, 1 December 1894, p. 3; *Hartlepool Northern Daily Mail*, 8 November 1894, p. 3; *Yorkshire Evening Press*, 8 November 1894, p. 4; *Yorkshire Post and Leeds Intelligencer*, 8 November 1894, p. 6. It seems likely, given that Annie is untraceable in the 1881 census, that she was living under the name of her tally husband. She indeed perhaps even viewed herself as married, for in the 1891 census, believing her son's father to have died in Australia, she listed her marital status as 'widow'. TNA, RG12/4012, f. 75, p. 14, s. 85, 1891 England, Wales & Scotland Census.

78 *East Anglian Daily Times*, 22 November 1900, p. 5; *Cambridge Daily News*, 22 November 1900, p. 3; *Cambridge Independent Press*, 17 March 1899, p. 5; TNA, RG12/1282, f. 56, p. 18, s. 103, 1891 England, Wales & Scotland Census.

79 *Halifax Guardian*, 24 December 1852, p. 5; TNA, HO107/2298, f. 107, p. 16, s. 76, 1851 England, Wales & Scotland Census.

80 TNA, RG10/4151, f. 115, p. 43, s. 236, 1871 England, Wales & Scotland Census.

81 *Burnley Express*, 7 January 1882, p. 6; Thane, 'Women and the Poor Law', 41.

82 TNA, RG11/4154, f. 128, p. 20, s. 1080, 1871 England, Wales & Scotland Census. As Jane Humphries notes in her study of female-headed households in early industrial Britain, 'The Poor Law operated not only to encourage widows and deserted wives to work full time but also get their children into employment. Poor relief was refused to families with children of an age the Guardians considered employable if they work not working.' Humphries, 'Female-Headed Households', 49–50.

83 *Burnley Express*, 7 January 1882, p. 6.

84 The prior census does not list her as having an occupation, but it does not necessarily mean she was not earning in some capacity during her

married life. TNA, RG11/1513, f. 7, p. 8, s. 492, 1881 England, Wales
& Scotland Census; *Oxford Chronicle and Reading Gazette*, 7 January
1888, p. 2.

85 *Leigh Chronicle & Weekly Advertiser*, 17 March 1882, p. 5; TNA,
RG09/2805, f. 56, p. 17, s. 86, 1861 England, Wales & Scotland Census;
TNA, RG10/3916, f. 54, p. 38, s. 194, 1871 England, Wales & Scotland
Census; TNA, RG11/3810, f. 56, p. 40, s. 466, 1881 England, Wales &
Scotland Census.

86 Yet as was commonplace in working-class communities during this
time, her meagre income did not prevent McKay from assisting neighbours in need. The inquest report revealed that McKay paid not only
her own rent but also regularly paid the rent 15d. a week for the two
orphaned youths that resided next door. The landlord 'would not let the
rent stay for a second week'. Therefore, having known their parents,
McKay felt duty-bound to assist them. The report also suggests that,
despite accruing arrears, McKay did not expect them to repay her. For
more information on support networks in working-class communities,
see Ross, 'Survival Networks', 4–27. *Express* (London), 23 December
1846, p. 3; *Hull Packet*, 18 December 1846, p. 5.

87 *Daily News* (London), 17 February 1870, p. 3.

2

The necessity for lodgings

When Mrs Mary Ann Allen started taking lodgers into her Burnley home, No. 17 Lomas Street, the men who arrived at her door were far from the usual candidates. Robert Chadwick, also known as Rothwell, had been born in Burnley and lived on Oxford Street, just a stone's from Lomas Street. Robert had been born illegitimate but was later recognised as the son of George Chadwick, the man with whom his mother had been 'boarding' at the time.[1] Married in his twenties, he established a home and shop on Oxford Street, but in his thirties, he lost everything following a prison sentence for defaulting on a fine imposed for assaulting his wife. Cast from the family home and reduced to hawking fish, Chadwick went in search of lodgings, residing at least at one other address before arriving at Allen's door.[2] The second of Allen's lodgers was William Crossley. Born in Burnley in 1850, Crossley, as a bachelor, had spent most of his twenties and thirties lodging in his hometown. However, it was widowhood that had brought him to Allen's door, having briefly been married to the woman with whom he had been lodging in 1890. When his wife died just eighteen months into their marriage, Crossley – along with his furniture – promptly took up new lodgings in Allen's home.[3] The third lodger was not native to Burnley, but neither was he an economic migrant, so to speak, at this point. Adam Robinson, a grocer's assistant, had arrived in Burnley in his twenties. As shop employees typically did, he appeared to have lived with his various employers for at least the next decade. By the early 1890s, however, while living under the roof of his latest employer on Trafalgar Street, Robinson left his employer's surveillance and moved into lodgings just one hundred yards away: Allen's home.[4]

The fourth lodger was known to his fellow lodgers only as 'Joe'. As he did not appear before the coroner's court investigating Allen's death, we cannot determine why he sought lodgings or, indeed, whether Joe was even his real name.[5]

If we knew little of the people who took lodgers into their homes, we know even less about those who sought lodgings. Most studies that venture into the domestic dwelling lodgings of Victorian England focus on those who accommodated lodgers rather than the lodgers themselves. Where lodgers are portrayed, they are 'semi-autonomous' young persons, typically male, between the stage of leaving home – often having migrated – and establishing a home of their own.[6] Indeed, at the turn of the twentieth century in Helsinki, Finland, the term 'young man' was synonymous with that of lodger.[7] Many of those lodgers present on the nights of the decennial censuses would fit such an archetypal trope of the lodger. As noted in the introduction to the book, the census enumerators employed by the office of the Registrar General in 1891 encountered 1,053,593 persons lodging or boarding in private residences (in other words, someone else's home),[8] 448,860 of those who were recorded being single males (aged sixteen upwards), including Adam Robinson who was, as noted above, boarding in the home of his employer. Yet young single males do not account for all those who sought lodgings in Victorian England. On that same census night, the enumerators encountered living as lodgers or boarders in domestic lodgings: 50,096 widowers, 30,072 married men, and 44,794 married men (spouse absent) – the latter figure including Robert Chadwick.[9]

The lodger population, however, was not just drawn from the male population, for the census enumerators also encountered 219,912 females (aged sixteen upwards) living as lodgers or boarders in other people's homes. Like the male lodging population, most female lodgers or boarders were single at the time of enumeration (125,988), accounting for over half of the female lodging population. Another 41,208 were widows. And, while you would expect an equal number of married women to men in lodgings, there were just 10,188 females reported as married. This discrepancy, fortunately, is easily accounted for as a mis-enumeration tied up with assumed gender roles at the time, for in some cases, where the men were recorded as 'lodger-head', their wives were often recorded as 'wives'. Therefore, when tallied, they fall beyond the category of 'lodger'. Such an error, however, would not occur when women were lodging without their spouses. Indeed, the number of married women lodging or boarding without their spouses was almost equal to that of men (38,944). 115,494 children (under sixteen years) were also enumerated as lodgers or boarders, who, as we will see below, sometimes lodged with their parent or parents but also, when tragedy struck, on their own.[10]

So, what do we know about all these different types of lodgers? In his study of family structure in the mid-nineteenth-century census, Michael Anderson hints at a more complex picture behind the who and the why of lodgings beyond that of the straightforward economic migrant. Anderson reveals that many lodgers in the industrial Lancashire town of Preston – with its economic opportunities in the textile trades – were young single male migrants, as indicated by their birthplace.[11] However, an unexpected revelation in Anderson's study is the number of non-migrants living as lodgers, as was the case with half of the lodgers living under Allen's roof. Among the single population living in lodgings, Anderson uncovered numerous adolescents and young adults with native status (i.e. born in the town). Attempting to piece together their story, Anderson speculates that such living situations resulted from parental mortality or outmigration rather than a deliberate decision to leave the parental home, except perhaps for those escaping turbulent homes or households headed by a 'badly off' father.[12]

Beyond the single lodger, Anderson also observed a significant portion of relatively young (under thirty-five years) married couples in lodgings, most of whom were from lower socioeconomic groupings – the lower factory workers, labourers, handloom weavers, and the unemployed. For this group in the early stages of marriage, low incomes, housing shortages, and high rental costs necessitated sharing a home with others. The path of lodging, Anderson suggests, was either taken because few other residential options were open to these couples who had migrated into town or, for non-migrant couples, mortality or birth rates had ruled out living with kin. Of course, Anderson explains, some non-migrant couples might also have made a deliberate decision not to live with kin. Yet whatever the reason, Anderson observes that by the time married couples embarked on family life, they had generally moved from lodgings to their own home.[13] According to Anderson, the next time a person might encounter lodgings was following the death of a spouse, or, as his data suggests, a male with no children to accommodate might move onto lodgings.[14] Nonetheless, the widower's tale – as evident in the life of William Crossley – was not necessarily a straightforward family lifecycle experience.

More recent census-based studies also locate a type of lodger absent in Anderson's sample or omitted in his discussion: the married lodger with spouse absent. Ruth McManus's investigation of Dublin's 1901 and 1911 census returns revealed that among the married persons in lodgings, a number – men in particular – were present without their spouses. Yet as McManus highlights, why such people lodged without their spouses cannot be answered through the census, speculating 'This may be due to the nature of their work, but is also possible that lodging was used in cases of marital breakdown', as evident with our own Robert Chadwick.[15] Likewise, Jeff Meek's study of boarding practice in early twentieth-century Scotland finds evidence in the 1911 Scottish census of married women boarding without their spouses. As with the men lodging without their wives, he suggests that seasonal or fixed-term employment that temporarily separated spouses drove wives into lodgings without their husbands. Moreover, lodgings could also provide a refuge, with Meek also suggesting that 'boarding offered a solution, albeit temporary, for women separated by threats of harm or marriage breakdown from their spouses'.[16]

Moving beyond the census, scholars of the long eighteenth century have identified other types of lodgers and the more personal stories behind their domestic arrangements. While most of the studies of the eighteenth-century lodger explore the experience of the more 'genteel' lodger and do not move beyond the metropolis, they nevertheless hint at some further types of lodgers drawn from the working classes and the less temporal lodgers. For example, Samantha K. Williams's study of petitions submitted to London's Foundling Hospital discusses how domestic servants – having fallen pregnant outside of marriage – fled to lodgings as their confinement approached.[17] In the same collection, Joanne McEwan, through a reading of legal narratives, identifies, among others, the 'perpetual lodger': persons who never established a home of their own but rather permanently lived in lodgings, such as our own Adam Robinson and, to some extent, Willliam Crossley.[18] As this book has shown thus far, legal narratives, namely the inquest reports, provide insights into the Victorian working-class accommodating lodgers. Likewise, they have much to reveal about Victorian working-class lodgers and the situations that drove them to lodgings. In this chapter, following the paper trail left by Victorian England working-class lodgers, starting with the inquest reports, we meet a range of persons for whom residing in lodgings became a necessity or choice and uncover their varying paths to lodging in someone else's home.

Single lodgers

As with the census, the inquest reports teem with young, single, migrant males – some from afar, some just a few miles from home – living in domestic dwelling lodgings, often on their route to settling permanently in the area with a home and family of their own (had it not been for their sudden death preventing them for continuing this trajectory). However, the inquest reports also pick up a different type of migrant lodger, one whose time in lodgings was just an annual occurrence rather than a permanent shift in location. Young single men and women often travelled far from home in the summer months in search of seasonal employment before returning home to their regular employment.[19] Where they found a home during these times has remained somewhat of a mystery, for the census – taken in March or early April – was explicitly scheduled to avoid recording such movement in the population.[20] But, as revealed in the inquest reports, seasonal migrants also sought lodgings and perhaps – somewhat like birds – returned to the same place each year. Chain makers Charlotte Whale and Sarah Ellen Proctor were two such young women who followed this route. In 1888, Whale and Proctor travelled together from their native Staffordshire, leaving behind their chain-making, to obtain seasonal employment in the market gardens of Isleworth. The journey, however, was no ad hoc adventure. Instead, it was one taken annually in spring, where they would arrive once again at the same lodgings, the home of married woman Ellen Callow.[21]

For those local adolescents earning a wage, by whatever means, lodging provided an alternative to the family home. At least twenty-four of the 139 lodgers that I have been able to identify as native were single and under thirty, but what prompted them to leave the familial home and seek lodgings? In some cases, wage-earning children found themselves turned out of the family home as a consequence of overcrowding.[22] However, throughout the inquest reports, parental death – as Anderson speculated – emerges as the prominent underlying reason for native adolescents to seek lodgings. Nonetheless, parental death and the adolescent's path to lodgings was not always a straightforward route. Within this also lay parental abandonment, outmigration, and family tension. Too young initially to support herself when her mother died in 1881, and with her father not in sight, Mary Ann McGarry initially found herself at the mercy of the Poor Law. Admitted to Leeds Moral and Industrial Training School, she would have begun training in a trade through which to support herself.[23] Yet her stay was a brief one. Within months, the twelve-year-old Mary Ann had found employment and moved into lodgings – her godmother's home.[24] For Clara Jones, the move to lodgings came not immediately after her father's death but after her bereaved mother decided to leave the family home in Newerne, Gloucestershire, and return to her native Monmouthshire. Her adolescent daughter, Clara, a washer at the local tin works, remained in Newerne and moved into lodgings. We can only speculate why Clara did not migrate with her mother. The inquest report into her death does hint at a romantic relationship that might have tethered Clara to Newerne, but it might also simply be the case that Clara – born in Newerne – did not want to leave the only home she had ever known.[25]

In other cases, family tensions were a contributing factor to children leaving the familial home and taking up lodgings after the death of a parent. The Hyde children had, by all accounts, suffered 'unceasing ill-usage' at the hands of their stepmother and been 'driven … away from her house to live in lodgings with kinder relations or more humane strangers'. The eldest daughter, Alice, a burler, was the first to escape the family home in Huddersfield, gone before even her fourteenth birthday. Following their father's suicide, the eldest son, Thomas, a teaser in one of Huddersfield's woollen mills, left when tensions came to a head following a dispute over laundry: 'I had not been in the house since.' The middle child, Hannah, a burler like her sister, went to 'live at James Bradbury's' shortly after. Only the youngest, John, remained under his stepmother's roof

– not, however, as her child, but rather – like his siblings – a lodger. As his stepmother informed the coroner's court investigating John's suicide – just two years after his father's own suicide – 'When his father died he (the deceased) was only a lodger to me, and I determined ... to do nothing for him.'[26]

Even where vice first appears to have driven young women into lodgings, it was parental death that seems to have placed them on this particular trajectory. Eliza Stanley had travelled just a short distance, crossing over the Thames from Slough to Clewer, maintaining herself through sex work. Notably, despite such a fall, this twenty-year-old native single woman was not entirely without kin, nor had she been abandoned by kin. As her father, Thomas Healey, reveals at the inquest into her death, which occurred after she returned to Slough and took lodgings there: 'She did not live at home with me. She lived at Slough-court, Slough, and had been leading an immoral life for about five years. I was in the habit of seeing her most days [and] She left home about five years ago.'[27] This departure, as England's death and burial records reveal, occurred shortly after the death of her mother. In a similarly parallel case in the Worcestershire town of Stourbridge, nineteen-year-old Mary Ann Perks was 'turned out of home by her father' shortly after her mother's death, after which she took up lodgings and 'got her living as best she could' – the implication being she had turned to sex work.[28]

McEwan observed that domestic dwelling lodgings also provided a convenient escape for unwed mothers approaching confinement. Surprisingly, however, only five such women appear in my sample of inquest reports. Less surprisingly, of the five, three were domestic servants. Twenty-three-year-old Clara Phillips, who had been living in service, typifies the image of the unmarried mother, of a young woman who leaves her position as a live-in servant as confinement approaches to find lodgings some distance away, concealing her condition from all those around her including those with whom she lodged.[29] Yet the inquest reports tell varying stories about the unmarried mother's path to lodgings, not always proceeding with a tale of rejection or abandonment. Single woman Elizabeth Saunders also left her place of service as she reached her confinement and went in search of lodgings in Exeter. However, in this instance, the woman with whom she lodged 'knew Saunders was *enceinte* and had been preparing for her confinement'. The deception came with the name she gave when she arrived at her lodgings, presenting herself as 'Mrs Balsdon', the wife of the man who lodged with her – unmarried tailor John Balsdon. He later admitted to the coroner, following Elizabeth's death in childbirth, that they were not married.[30] On the other hand, Mary Ann Melton knew of her single female lodger's approaching confinement but – as noted in Chapter 1 – she could not turn her away because she depended on the income from lodgers to pay her rent after being deserted by her husband.[31]

For most single lodgers, natives and migrants, living in lodgings was a brief domestic interlude – one taken before marriage and setting up a home. The surviving Hyde children married and went on to form their own home just a few years after leaving the family home for lodgings.[32] And this certainly would have been the case for twenty-two-year-old Cornishman William Hocking had he not been killed in an accident in a Carn Brea mine just a stone's throw from where he was born. The inquest reports states that he was 'a lodger at the time of his death with Martha George, but who was about to get married'.[33] But not all those who took up lodgings in late adolescence and young adulthood took the route to marriage. William Crossley was one such lodger until his very brief marriage late in life. Crossley's reason for leaving home and taking up lodgings is somewhat hazy, but we know he had lived a somewhat itinerant and erratic existence in his hometown. The inquest report regarding Mrs Mary Ann Allen's murder at the hands of Crossley – a story we will return to in Chapter 5 – recorded that Crossley had gone from job to job, having 'latterly carried on the occupation of a labourer at Messrs. Butterworth and Dickinson's foundry, Trafalgar-street … He was originally a spinner, but subsequently became engaged as a manservant in public-houses, serving in that capacity at various places, but ultimately entering into the service of Councillor D.D. Dickinson, of Waterloo Hotel, Trafalgar Street.'[34] Crossley's residential circumstances mirrored his haphazard employment history. Despite 'relatives of his living in the same locality', Crossley spent his adult life moving between lodgings.[35]

Other perpetual lodgers carved out a more stable lodging arrangement, albeit occasionally interrupted by death. Cotton mill operative John Hampson spent his entire adult life lodging in other people's homes in the Lancashire market town of Tyldesley with Shakerley, where he had been born and bred. When he was around seventeen years old, Hampson's father died, forcing him to promptly find lodgings in the Charles Street home of Alice Brimlow – a detail uncovered at an inquest held in 1882 regarding the death of another resident where Hampson testified that 'he [himself] had lodged in the house ... for 17 years'.[36] When Alice Brimlow died four years later, Hampson left his home of two decades and sought new lodgings. By the 1891 census, he had settled in the Ash Street home of fifty-five-year-old widow Hannah Smith and was still lodging there in 1901. Hampson likely remained in Smith's house until her death before coming to lodge with Ann Alldred.[37] Alldred's husband died as a result of an accident at work during the same quarter as Hannah Smith's death, and with three children to maintain, it became necessary to take a lodger, which, as the 1911 census shows, was John Hampson.[38] Once again, Hampson establishes (nearly) two-decades-long lodgings. However, in this instance, this was with the same family rather than the same householder, for he eventually came to lodge with Alldred's married daughter, Edna, on Wood Street.[39] When he died in 1927, aged seventy-nine, John Hampson had spent over sixty years as a domestic dwelling lodger.

Of course, men like Hampson dominated the sphere of perpetual lodging. Yet while we know of the benefits for men living in lodgings as boarders (as most did) – having all their domestic needs met without the responsibility of maintaining a home and family – the inquest reports are relatively silent on whether choice or circumstance brought about this particular domestic arrangement. In other words, did men such as John Hampson, who spent their lives in lodgings, shun marriage, or had they been unlucky in love? For Adam Robinson, at least, employment had carved out his route to perpetual lodgerdom. Arriving in Burnley in his twenties to work as a grocer's assistant, he spent many years living under his employer's roof before oscillating between lodging at work and domestic dwelling lodgings. However, those formative years spent under his employer's roof made him a less viable candidate for marriage. As Christopher P. Hosgood contends, male shop assistants living under the control of their employers, told 'when to rise, when to sleep, when to eat, when to pray, and what to wear', were left emasculated, and their chances of marriage significantly reduced.[40] Moreover, Robinson may have never established earnings befitting a male breadwinner, further hindering his chances of setting up a home. Robinson remained on a shop assistant's wage even as he entered middle age. Living in several domestic dwelling lodgings in the 1890s undoubtedly brought him personal freedom, but by 1901, Robinson returned to lodging with an employer.[41] However, as old age set in, Robinson was again in domestic lodgings. By 1911, he had settled in the home of labourer John Sturdy and his family as their boarder and remained with them for at least the next decade. However, living as he did provided little safety net, for when he died in 1927, aged seventy, the address where his death took place – Briercliffe Road – was the location of Burnley's work-house.[42] Perpetual lodgerdom, it seems, had brought Robinson, at least, a pauper's death.

Married lodgers

Lodging, however, was more than just the domain of single persons. At least 149 lodgers in my sample were married. Many fit the pattern of newlyweds not yet able to establish a home of their own. For others, however, starting married life in someone else's home meant never establishing their own home. Following their marriage, Oxford labourer Christopher John Chesterman and his wife Mercy did not have the means to establish a home. Instead, they took up lodgings in their hometown. Yet theirs was not a straightforward case of having no kin to turn to for accommodation, nor was lodging for them a mere passage in their married life. As I will explore in more detail in the next chapter, after living as lodgers in the home of Mercy's sister, Mary Burdock (née Webb, Sloper), records suggest that the Chestermans never established their own home.[43] Instead, they spent their married life living with other relatives. Their residential choice was perhaps shaped by the fact they never begot children.[44] Indeed, only six married couples in my sample had children, but these were not couples starting out on family life.

The same reasons that compelled married couples with children to take in lodgers were also the very reasons that forced some families to leave their homes and seek lodgings. As seen in Chapter 1, married couples who spiralled into illness and poverty took in lodgers to keep the roof over their heads. When such an option was not viable, families were forced from their homes and into lodgings, if not the workhouse. When steel forge labourer Thomas Brannan and Maria McArthur married in Sheffield in late 1877, they already had two children, and by 1881, the census shows them in a home of their own, No. 9 Peacroft.[45] But, just over a year later, the family – now including three children – had given up their home and moved into lodgings, a garret in a neighbouring house. Here, the family continued to grow with the arrival of at least two more children, further straining Brannan's wages. Six years later, the family was still lodging in the garret when Maria and their youngest child died. But how did the Brannan family become trapped into lodgings if so many other large working-class families just about kept the roof over their heads? The answer is one of health. Both Thomas and Maria, the inquest reports show, suffered from poor health that impacted their ability to earn. When Thomas Brannan presented himself before Sheffield's coroner's court investigating his wife's death, reporters observed that despite only being thirty-six years of age, 'trouble and privation have prematurely aged him, and he presents a sorry sight'. Brannan went on to inform the court of the family's struggles. Finding himself out of work some months before his wife's death, he alone entered the workhouse so that 'his children might have some support', the guardians permitting 6s. of outdoor relief a week for his wife in exchange for his indoor labour. His wife – 'a weakly woman' – could not work and contribute to the family purse. Indeed, as Maria's health declined, she became increasingly dependent on the 'kindness' of her neighbours. Eventually, however, Maria succumbed to heart disease, which the jury concurred was 'no doubt accelerated by want of proper food'.[46]

For some families, however, their time in lodgings was so brief as to have gone unrecorded if not for a coroner's inquest. The position of Camberwell-born greengrocer Charles Holmes, if one was to trust the census entirely, was as the head of his own home following his marriage in 1889, despite the ebbs and flows in his occupations signalling both a rise and fall in household fortunes. On the night of the census 1891, Charles was recorded as a general dealer, residing with his wife Annie and their two-year-old daughter in a four-roomed cottage on West Road, Teddington.[47] Ten years later, now with three children, Charles was reduced to the earnings of a flower seller and the occupant of a house on the Uxbridge Road, albeit one absented by his hospitalised wife.[48] Holmes's ability to maintain a home in the face of occupational decline would remain undisputed had it not been for a fatal fire that ripped through the Teddington home of bootmaker Frederick Hall in 1900, consuming the lives of two of the Holmes's children. The children were present in Hall's house because, it transpired, the entire family were living in Hall's home as lodgers. We do not know precisely when the family – now including four children – had to give up their own home, but we do learn that on moving into Hall's home they took the two top back rooms, and it was here that they became trapped in a fire. Mrs Smith, injured from her jump to safety, was conveyed to a hospital for surgery, explaining her absence from the family home in 1901.[49]

The census also suggests that Oxford shoemaker Thomas Harris spent his married life – even as he moved into old age – as the head of his own home.[50] When Thomas Harris died in 1876, just under five years after the last census, we might assume he had died under his own roof. Yet an inquest report into his death at the age of sixty-four in February 1876 tells a different story of the domestic arrangements in the final years of his life. Called before the coroner, college servant William Matthews stated that he lived at No. 2 Howard Street, Cowley, and '[Thomas Harris] and his wife have lodged at my house since July [1874].' The inquest report then reveals that old age, reduced earnings, and drink were deciding factors in the couple's move to lodgings. Witness Joseph Carpenter, the landlord of the Maudlin Arms, informed the court that Harris 'was in the habit of comings to his [public] house' to tout for business – enquiring, for example, with Carpenter's lodger 'if he could find him some work, and had a pair of boots given him to mend' and then drinking what little money he earned.[51]

However, almost a third (twenty-four men, twenty women) of married persons living as lodgers in someone else's home were not in their marital unit.[52] As McManus and Meek speculate and the inquest reports confirm, most of those lodging without their spouse were doing so due to marital breakdown. Unpacking the inquest reports to reveal more about the maritally separated spouse's path to lodgings, it becomes evident that estranged husbands living in lodgings had breached the acceptable norms of behaviour within working-class marriage. In Victorian working-class society, there was an expectation for wives to tolerate bad marriages. Yet there clearly came tipping points when the husband – the head of the household – could find himself ejected from the family home. For some of these husbands, lodgings were only a pitstop before returning to their forgiving wives. For example, Nottingham framesmith James Foster spent some time going back and forth between his marital home and lodgings as his marriage deteriorated. In 1879, when Foster attempted suicide and was subsequently charged, his wife Ann pleaded with the judge 'if she was compelled to live with him, as she had forgiven him for illtreating her many times' and he was in 'the habit of drinking all his life'.[53] Despite the judge encouraging her to allow her husband to return to the family home, he only briefly returned home in 1881 – resident with his wife and children on census night – before he was again turned out and once again went into lodgings.[54]

At least two of the maritally separated men (though still legally married) living in lodgings had served prison sentences relating to domestic abuse. Thomas Morris – *alias* Nash – in his forties and jeweller by trade, was living in the London Borough of Clerkenwell without his wife and family. Having been tried and sentenced to six months imprisonment with hard labour for 'cruelly assaulting' his wife and 'violating his daughter', upon his release, he was permanently banned from his family home. Moving into lodgings, he paid his way through the occasional work he undertook in his trade.[55] Burnley man, Robert Chadwick, likewise moved into lodgings upon his release from prison. In 1882, Chadwick married Emma Roberts and established a home and a fruit and fish business on Oxford Road, followed shortly after that by the birth of their three children. Less than a decade later, the marriage ended following Chadwick's gaol sentence for defaulting on a court fine imposed after he assaulted his wife while in a heavily intoxicated state. On his release, finding that his 'furniture and stock-in-trade [had been] sold under distraint', Chadwick was a reduced man, working as a fish hawker, earning 16s. to 20s. a week and living as a lodger, in the first instance, with his step-sister.[56] And, as we know, Chadwick eventually found board and lodgings with Mrs Mary Ann Allen and was witness to her horrific murder. Yet when Robert Chadwick took up lodgings with Mrs Mary Ann Allen, he was no longer alone. He was now accompanied by his two surviving children – James, aged ten, and Lincoln, aged nine.[57] Although, with their mother still living and no other explanation as to their presence, we can only speculate why they now lived with their father. Certainly, their presence in lodgings with their father was not the norm.

Some maritally separated men found a sense of permanency, even home, in domestic dwelling lodgings. Indeed, several such men lodged in the same house for years before they became the witness or subject of a coroner's inquest, suggesting a decision to remain as a lodger rather than live in adulterous cohabitation with another. For example, following a marital breakdown, sixty-one-year-old Oxford basket-maker George Lewis settled as a lodger in the home of widow Charlotte Arnold, where he died three years later.[58] Likewise, in Sunderland, having separated from his wife in his mid-thirties, cabinet maker James Lee came to No. 14 George Street as a lodger, remaining there for the next eight years – and probably would have done so for many more years if not killed in suspicious circumstances at the age of forty-seven.[59] Certainly, for some men, at least domestically, there was little motivation for entering another romantic cohabitation when they could have all their domestic needs – food, washing, and attendance – supplied by the woman with whom they lodged, as I will return to in Chapter 3.

By way of contrast, in the event of marital breakdown, wives did not typically follow the path to lodgings. Instead, as evidenced in Chapter 1, where there were still dependent children, estranged wives laboured hard to maintain the family home. It might have also been the case that householders were perhaps more reluctant to accommodate a maritally separated woman with children than a male who had relinquished his family responsibilities. Nonetheless, lodgings provided an escape route for some working-class wives, but the inquest reports reveal they were often not on their own. Among twenty married women living in lodgings without their legal husband, at least a quarter are confirmed as lodging with a partner to whom they were not married. In June 1840, a young, apparently married couple, going by the name of Southam, took up lodgings in the Leamington home of Jane Crump. Only one of the parties, however, was legally married. Elizabeth, whose legal name was Varney, had been abandoned by her husband shortly after their marriage. Nonetheless, any relationship she went on to form after the desertion would mean living in adultery, which is just what she did when she established a relationship with car driver William Southam.[60]

Cases of adulterous cohabitation in lodgings continued throughout the Victorian period. Indeed, my sample yields three such cases in London in 1894 alone. The first, Mrs Hailes, eloped with her lodger in April, with the couple moving into lodgings just off the Old Kent Road.[61] Two months later, Mrs Mary Elizabeth Smith, some months advanced in pregnancy, left her husband and home in Paddington to elope with the couple's former lodger, finding lodgings together in Walthamstow. Yet attached to their arrival at lodgings was a necessary deception. Like the unmarried mothers that had come before them, adulterous couples had a better chance of obtaining lodgings if they passed as married. Called to testify at the inquest into Mrs Smith's death, widow Annette Brown stated that the couple had 'hired a furnished bedroom off her four or five weeks ago'. Asked by the coroner, 'You thought they were married?' Brown responded, 'Yes, I did; and she seemed such a nice sort of woman.'[62] And in June that year, after twenty-six-year-old Ellen Round, wife of a boot repairer, began an intimate relationship with a man named John Hampton, they fled to lodgings where they presented themselves as Mr. and Mrs. Freeman. Yet when the deception was uncovered, lodgers living in adulterous cohabitation could promptly face eviction. Householders generally did not want trouble under their roof. The 'Southams'' 1840s sojourn into lodgings was to be short-lived. Within the fortnight, Crump 'heard they were not married and gave them notice to quit'. Likewise, when Round's husband tracked the couple down, he revealed to the householder, Ann Pollard, the true nature of the 'Freemans'' relationship, to which Pollard responded, 'You had better take her home, for she cannot stop here.'[63]

The inquest reports also reveal that marital breakdown does not explain all the circumstances of married persons residing as lodgers with spouses absent. As discussed above, Maria Brannan's husband was not living in their lodgings at the time of her death, having entered the workhouse to support his family. Yet whereas the Brannan family were already living in lodgings, the institutionalisation of a spouse could also trigger a move into lodgings. For men in particular, where there were no daughters to provide domestic support, lodgings answered the question as to who would do for him. For example, when the wife of Chesterfield waggon-builder William Petheram was committed to Derby County Lunatic Asylum, he clearly did not expect her to return, for he soon 'sold up' and asked his neighbour, Elizabeth Houseley 'to take him as a lodger, and she did so'. Petheram's sojourn in her home, however, was but a brief one. The following month – at the age of fifty-six – he was found drowned.[64] Not all, however, were so keen to take up lodgings in the absence of a spouse. When the wife of Barnsley labourer John Lockwood was committed to Wadsley Asylum, the sexagenarian endeavoured to maintain their home through the assistance of his neighbour, Mrs Martha Wild. Nonetheless, despite Lockwood's determination that 'he should keep a house for himself as long as he could', as his health declined, he conceded that he could no longer maintain his home. Visiting the Wild's home, Lockwood 'talked for a considerable time, and after jocularly asking if she would take him as a lodger'. But Lockwood never did move into Wild's home, for just a few hours later, Martha found him hanging from his staircase.[65]

In contrast, a married person might seek lodgings for their ailing spouse. The workhouse and the public asylum instilled dread among the Victorians, and lodgings – as I will discuss in more detail in Chapter 3 – provided an alternative to such feared committals. Nonetheless, such a domestic arrangement could still see married couples parted. As Martha Evans's health declined in her fifties, becoming, as the inquest report describes, 'paralytic' and 'subject to a deranged state of mind', she and her husband, hairdresser George Evans, travelled from their home in Liverpool to Wadswick, Wiltshire – Martha's native home – to seek lodgings. Yet only one of them was to remain. Having found Martha lodgings with the Jordan family, for whom he was to pay for bed, board, and care, George departed to London in search of work and, most likely, lodgings. He was never to see Martha again.[66]

Widowed lodgers

Death was a frequent and destructive figure in the working-class home. As we have seen above, parental death paved the way for adolescents to seek lodgings in the place that they called home. Similarly, surviving spouses could find themselves compelled into lodgings where the strains that came with the loss of a spouse were too much to bear, with the inquest sample revealing at least thirty-eight widowers and thirty-eight widows living as lodgers following spousal loss. For young widowers, as I have shown elsewhere, the death of a wife brought acute domestic strain. Where children needed to be cared for, they might promptly remarry. Meanwhile, other young widowers, releasing themselves from the burden of supporting a household, might leave their children with relatives and move into lodgings. And, while some of the relatively young lodger-widowers eventually went on to remarry, others joined their single counterparts as perpetual lodgers, such as Northampton shoe packer Walter Jones, who, widowed before his thirty-sixth birthday, spent the rest of his life (a further ten years) lodging on the Wellingborough Road.[67] Older widowers, on the other hand, with no children in tow, would turn to lodgings when other domestic options had been exhausted, such as, as we have seen, assistance from their own female lodgers or neighbours.[68]

For widows, the loss of the male breadwinner brought the financial burden of maintaining a home down on their own shoulders. As we witnessed in Chapter 1, some widows – accommodating lodgers and undertaking an array of domestic labours – toiled tirelessly to keep the roof over their heads. However, other widows – through choice or necessity – gave up their marital homes and moved into lodgings. When Caroline Watton married smith-journeyman William Marks in 1850 in their home parish of St Luke's, Middlesex, the couple first shared a home in George's Yard with widowed pot scourer Frances Hatfield and Hatfield's unwed brother.[69] Eventually, they settled in a neighbouring property, but in 1863, Caroline's husband died during an outbreak of typhus fever in the neighbourhood. Three years later, she returned to Hatfield's home as her lodger.[70] Notably, with no record of the Marks ever begetting children, Caroline Marks would have had no difficulty obtaining lodgings when she moved from her home.

Children certainly complicated the young widow's move into lodgings. In a life marked by poverty, Colchester widow Deborah Willis had to make difficult decisions when she could no longer maintain the roof over her children's heads. Married to a shoemaker, the couple – as evidenced by the shoemakers we met in Chapter 1 – would have struggled to provide for their children. Unsurprisingly then, when her husband died, Willis rapidly fell into destitution. Indeed, in this dire situation, she turned to sex work.

Eventually, unable to maintain her family, Willis admitted four of her children into the workhouse. She did not, however, enter herself. Instead, with her youngest child, she took up lodgings where she died, aged just thirty, 'from a low fever, produced ... by her mode of living and the state she was in'.[71] On the other hand, Eliza Leaver had led a relatively comfortable life in her Oxford home before the death of her husband. Having, as seen in Chapter 1, moved to a larger house so they had the space for lodgers to help sustain themselves in old age, Eliza soon found herself a widow. Eliza managed to maintain her home through lodgers for some time, but when her most dependable lodger died, she was forced to give up the home when the Poor Law authorities refused any more assistance bar the workhouse. Taking up lodgings, she died shortly after, and 'not a penny was found in the room'.[72]

But why did these bereaved women end up in lodgings rather than in the homes of kin, as was the typically expected route for widows? Quite simply, they had no kin to turn to in their time of need. Caroline Marks's parents were – unsurprisingly, given the mortality rates at this time – both long since deceased by the time she was widowed in her late thirties, and she appeared to have no other kin in the area. Similarly, at the inquest into her death, it was noted that Willis's 'father had been dead a long time, and ... she has [no] relatives in the town except a daughter-in-law'.[73] Meanwhile, Eliza Leaver, having never begotten children, lacked the safety net that adult children could provide as their parents' health and wealth deteriorated in old age. Yet not all the older widows living in lodgings lacked this safety net but instead had chosen, or in some cases were forced, to take lodgings rather than live with kin. When monthly out-pensioner, eighty-four-year-old Mary Corker, came to reside with her daughter at No. 2 Chesterfield Street, Marylebone, tensions grew between mother and daughter. Following a 'serious quarrel ... concerning some family matters', Mary left her daughter's home and headed to the workhouse. However, 'as she had only the week before received her monthly pension', she could not be admitted that week and had to seek temporary lodgings.[74] Widower Owen Girdlestone, a former tailor, had first found a home with his adult son but was forced to seek lodgings after his increasingly volatile behaviour saw him cast out by his son. As his son told the coroner's court investigating his father's suicide: 'I was obliged to send him away in consequence of his coming home so often in drink.' However, his father did not go too far. Finding lodgings less than a mile away, he continued to return to his son's home when intoxicated.[75]

Keeping widowed kin at a distance by placing them in lodgings or, indeed, the widowed kin themselves keeping their distance by taking up lodgings did not always signal family tensions. When widow Elizabeth Allen (also known as Elizabeth Stanley) moved from her home in the Buckinghamshire village Marsh Gibbon to North End, Buckingham, soon after the death of her husband, she took up residence with her son, William.[76] Yet within the decade, Elizabeth, now in her seventies, had become a lodger in the home of labourer Robert Howard. We do not know why Elizabeth moved out of the home of her kin into lodgings. Perhaps, with William's family growing, there became an increasing need to separate older children into differing sleeping quarters, resulting in no bed for her to sleep on. What we know is that Elizabeth had not gone far, just ten or fifteen minutes away, and when she fell ill, her daughter-in-law soon arrived to assist.[77] Meanwhile, seventy-two-year-old widowed carpenter and joiner Curtis George might have died in lodgings, but it soon transpired he was far from alone. Having 'long ceased to work', he 'maintained entirely by his children', one of whom – an adult son – lived directly next door to his father's lodgings. The son had perhaps himself sought the lodgings for his ageing father.[78]

Conclusion

The domestic dwelling lodgers of Victorian working-class England rarely fit into the existing trope of the lodger. Of course, I do not deny that young single persons, usually male, made up the majority of lodgers at this time. Rather, I have demonstrated that like the lodgers of No. 17 Lomas Street, England's domestic dwelling lodgers were as varied as the divergent paths that had brought them to the doors of those who accommodated lodgers. Domestic dwelling lodgings were not just a stop-gap for young single migrant men on their way to marriage but also a source of temporary, if not permanent, shelter for non-migrant single, married, and widowed persons – male and female – whose home lives had been dismantled by financial difficulties and domestic tragedies. Through the inquest reports, I have provided further evidence to Anderson's argument that parental death compelled young non-migrants into lodgings. However, the inquest reports also reveal that in many cases, parental death alone was not enough in itself to force a move to lodgings. Instead, in nearly all cases, family tensions played a significant role in such a move. Indeed, family tensions could also go a long way to explaining the presence of older widows and widowers in lodgings. However, it was more likely in many of these cases that adult children could not, rather than would not, accommodate their ageing parents.

I have also demonstrated in this chapter that the working-class married population could find themselves compelled into domestic dwelling lodgings. Alongside the newlyweds' brief sojourn in lodging, married couples could find themselves in lodgings at any stage of the marital lifecycle when financial hardship hit. In most cases, their time in lodgings was but fleeting as to almost be missed by the historical record. Though, for couples unable to get back on their feet, lodgings were just one step closer to the workhouse. Yet we must not assume all those married persons living in lodgings did so in their legal conjugal union. Confirming McManus and Meek's suggestion, marital breakdown was the overwhelming cause of lone spouses living in lodgings. However, among these separated spouses stands out a distinct gender difference, for while the maritally separated male tended to arrive at lodgings alone, the maritally separated female was generally in company. However, it was not her children with whom she arrived, but rather her lover who – as I return to in Chapter 5 – in some cases had been her lodger.

Finally, as the legal narratives show for the long eighteenth century, there were those among the Victorian working class for whom lodging was not a temporary recourse: the bachelor. Yet while living in lodgings meant having their domestic needs met without the financial responsibility of maintaining their own home, it is still difficult to determine whether perpetual lodgings was a chosen path or one carved out by the vicissitudes of life. Moving forward to the next chapter, having met now those who took in lodgers and the lodgers themselves, I explore the process of finding lodgers and lodgings – where neighbours, friends, and kin all played a crucial role – and the navigation of the lodging agreement.

Notes

1 TNA, RG09/3066, f. 81, p. 19, s. 77, 1861 England, Wales & Scotland Census.

2 *Burnley Express*, 17 May 1890, p. 7; *Burnley Express*, 20 September 1890, p. 6; *Burnley Express*, 14 July 1894, p. 8. In the 1891 census, Robert – listed under the name of Chadwick – was a lodger with Emanuel Collinge and Sarah Collinge, which, as the prior newspaper reports reveal, was the home of his brother-in-law/step-sister. TNA, RG12/3365, f. 117, 62, s. 350, 1891 England, Wales & Scotland Census.

3 On the night of the 1881 census, Crossley – employed at the time as a cotton mule spinner – was lodging on Keppel Street, Habergham Eaves, with the Green family. TNA, RG11/4151, f. 97, p. 19, s. 859, 1881 England, Wales & Scotland Census. On the night of the 1891 census, William Crossley – employed as a servant – was lodging in the Sandygate home of the Standings. However, shortly after, he went to lodge in the home of Sarah Bowes and by the end of that same year, they were married. TNA, RG12/3368, f. 119, p. 25, s. 170, 1891 England, Wales & Scotland Census; *Burnley Express*, 13 June 1894, p. 3.

4 On the night of the 1881 census, aged twenty-seven years at the time, he was living as an 'assistant' in the home of his employer, grocer Alfred Dickinson. By the 1891 census, where he was listed as a 'boarder', Robinson had moved to Trafalgar Street, taking up a home and working with his employer, greengrocer James Blackburn. TNA, RG11/4149, f. 153, p. 26, s. 1354, 1881 England, Wales & Scotland Census; TNA, RG12/3367, f. 115, p. 7, s. 47, 1891 England, Wales & Scotland Census.

5 *Burnley Express*, 16 June 1894, p. 8.

6 Leonore Davidoff, 'The Separation of Home and Work? Landladies and Lodgers in Nineteenth-and Twentieth-Century England', in Sandra Burman (ed.), *Fit Work for Women* (London: Croom Helm, 1979), pp. 78–9.

7 Though Moring also observes that while this was the case in Helsinki, in Tampere – where there was a high demand for female labour – 68.6 per cent of lodgers were female women. Most of these fell into the age category of twenty to twenty-nine years, pp. 53–5. Beatrice Moring, 'Gender,

Class and Lodging in Urban Finland Around 1900', *Continuity and Change*, 31:1 (2016), 53–5, 58. DOI: 10.1017/S0268416016000102.

8 In 56,998 cases, the sex of the lodger/boarder is unknown, while in 77,751 cases, the age of the lodger/boarder is unknown.

9 A further seven men were enumerated as divorced, while in 9,609 cases, the enumerators could not determine the male lodger or boarder's marital status.

10 All census data gathered is from Kevin Schürer and Edward Higgs, Integrated Census Microdata (I-CeM), 1851–1911. [data collection]. UK Data Service. SN: 7481 (2020). DOI: 10.5255/UKDA-SN-7481-2.

11 Michael Anderson, *Family Structure in Nineteenth Century Lancashire* (Cambridge: Cambridge University Press, 1971), pp. 53–4.

12 Anderson, *Family Structure*, pp. 53–5, 124–9, 131.

13 Anderson, *Family* Structure, pp. 49–53.

14 Anderson, *Family Structure*, p. 50. Notably, the higher proportion of older widowed men in lodgings compared to their female counterparts is far from universal. For example, Moring's study of Finnish lodgers found that female lodgers aged fifty years and over outnumbered male lodgers by three to one. Moring, 'Gender, Class and Lodging', 60.

15 Ruth McManus, 'Dublin's Lodger Phenomenon in the Early Twentieth Century', *Irish Economic and Social History*, 45:1 (2018), 34. DOI: 10.1177/0332489318801622.

16 Jeff Meek, 'Boarding and Lodging Practices in Early Twentieth-Century Scotland', *Continuity and Change*, 31:1 (2016), 93. DOI: 10.1017/S0268416016000084.

17 Samantha K. Williams, '"I Was Forced to Leave My Place to Hide My Shame": The Living Arrangements of Unmarried Mothers in London in the Early Nineteenth Century', in Joanne McEwan and Pamela Sharpe (eds), *Accommodating Poverty: The Housing and Living Arrangements of the English Poor, c. 1600–1850* (Basingstoke: Palgrave Macmillan, 2011), pp. 203–12.

18 Joanne McEwan, 'The Lodging Exchange: Space, Authority and Knowledge in Eighteenth-Century London', in Joanne McEwan and Pamela Sharpe (eds), *Accommodating Poverty: The Housing and Living Arrangements of the English Poor, c. 1600–1850* (Basingstoke: Palgrave Macmillan, 2011), p. 52.

19 Davidoff, 'The Separation of Home and Work', p. 80.

20 As Leonore Davidoff notes, the night on which the census was taken – falling either in March or the beginning of April – intentionally excluded a whole range of people who sought lodging after travelling to the area for seasonal employment. Davidoff, 'The Separation of Home and Work', p. 81.

21 *Isleworth Echo* (London), 20 April 1888, p. 4. Court records place Charlotte Whale in Middlesex, August 1887 – charged with assault, latterly found innocent. *Middlesex Independent*, 3 August 1887, p. 3.

22 Vicky Holmes, 'Accommodating the Lodger: The Domestic Arrangements of Lodgers in Working-Class Dwellings in a Victorian Provincial Town', *Journal of Victorian Culture*, 19:3 (2014), 322–4. DOI: 10.1080/13555502.2014.947181.

23 Derek Fraser, *A History of Modern Leeds* (Manchester: Manchester University Press, 1980), p. 233.

24 Mary Ann was listed as an inmate of the school on census night 1881, but – by her own account – she had left by June. With her mother's death having taken place in the last quarter of 1880, Mary Ann would have spent less than a year as an inmate before moving on. TNA, RG11/4524, f. 126, p. 8, s. 911, 1881 England, Wales & Scotland Census; *Leeds Times*, 25 February 1882, p. 2.

25 TNA, RG09/3978, f. 65, p. 19, s. 82, 1861 England, Wales & Scotland Census; *Gloucester Journal*, 20 February 1864, p. 3.

26 *Leeds Mercury*, 15 July 1858, p. 1; *Huddersfield Chronicle*, 17 July 1858, p. 8.

27 Herein lies another issue with the census and, indeed, registration records. Born in 1864, Eliza was registered in her mother's name, Stanley. No father is recorded. Turning to the next census record, 1871, we find the Stanleys – a widowed mother and two daughters – residing in Slough Court. Also present was their lodger, thirty-five-year-old brickmaker Thomas Haley. TNA, RG10/1401, f. 26, p. 50, s. 286, 1871 England, Wales & Scotland Census. By 1881, Eliza was living in lodgings. TNA RG11/1324, f. 103, p. 14, s. 825, 1881 England, Wales & Scotland Census; *Windsor & Eton Express*, 12 January 1884, p. 4.

28 *County Advertiser & Herald for Staffordshire and Worcestershire*, 25 February 1888, p. 3; TNA, RG11/2886, f. 101, p. 26, s. 789, 1881 England, Wales & Scotland Census. Her mother Phoebe died in the last quarter of 1886.

29 *Hampshire Independent*, 18 May 1864, p. 3.

30 *Western Times*, 21 January 1888, p. 3; *Western Morning News*, 19 January 1888, p. 8.

31 *Norfolk Chronicle*, 18 December 1858, p. 6; *Norwich Mercury*, 18 December 1858, p. 6.

32 In 1860, Alice married joiner and cabinet maker Mark Wilkinson, and by 1861, they were living as a family in Stainland with Old Lindley, TNA, RG09/3288, f. 112, p. 28, s. 126, 1861 England, Wales & Scotland Census. Thomas, now employed as a slubber, marries the following year and sets up home in Lindley. TNA, RG10/4381, f. 33, p. 20,

s. 104, 1871 England, Wales & Scotland Census. Hannah, having gone into domestic service, died – unmarried – in 1865. TNA, RG09/3273, f. 22, p. 1, s. 3, 1861 England, Wales & Scotland Census.

33 *Cornish Telegraph*, 8 June 1864, p. 2.

34 *Burnley Express*, 13 June 1894, p. 3.

35 *Burnley Express*, 13 June 1894, p. 3.

36 *Leigh Chronicle & Weekly Advertiser*, 17 March 1882, p. 5.

37 TNA, RG12/3092, f. 137, p. 17, s. 89, 1891 England, Wales & Scotland Census; TNA, RG13/3597, f. 74, p. 23, s. 139, 1901 England, Wales & Scotland Census.

38 *Leigh Chronicle and Weekly District Advertiser*, 29 May 1908, 2. TNA, RG14/23246, s. 53, 1911 England, Wales & Scotland Census.

39 TNA, RG15/18473, s. 369, 1921 England, Wales & Scotland Census.

40 Christopher P. Hosgood, '"Mercantile Monasteries": Shops, Shop Assistants, and Shop Life in Late-Victorian and Edwardian Britain', *Journal of British Studies*, 38:3 (1999), 331–9. DOI: 10.1086/386197. Ruth McManus's study of lodging in Dublin also observes a category of lodgers who 'lodged' with their employers. McManus, 'Dublin's Lodger Phenomenon', 33.

41 *Burnley Express*, 14 July 1894, p. 8.

42 *Burnley Express*, 29 October 1927, p. 18.

43 *Oxfordshire Weekly News*, 15 August 1888, p. 2.

44 TNA, RG12/1168, f. 80, p. 9, s. 46, 1891 England, Wales & Scotland Census. In 1891, the couples were living with relatives, as relatives rather than lodgers. Only when Mercy's husband died in 1896, and she formed a relationship with house painter Benjamin Chesney, does Mercy appear to have finally stopped living under other people's roofs. TNA, RG13/1384, f. 51, p. 21, s. 151, 1901 England, Wales & Scotland Census. On census night, 1901, living on English Row, Mercy – listed as a widow – is the head of her home, with Chesney listed as a visitor.

45 This case is also a clear example of misrepresentations in the census enumerators' books. Married in 1877, and their three children born between 1875 and 1881 registered as the couple's children, it emerges that on the night of the 1881 census, while Thomas Brennan – as the head of the household – is listed as married, Maria – under her maiden name and her marital status as single – is listed as a servant, a housekeeper, to Thomas. TNA, RG11/4646, f. 79, p. 9, s. 638, 1881 England, Wales & Scotland Census.

46 *Sheffield Daily Telegraph*, 6 March 1888, p. 3; *Sheffield Evening Telegraph*, 6 March 1888, p. 4.

47 TNA, RG12/618, f. 9, p. 11, s. 81, 1891 England, Wales & Scotland Census.

48 TNA, RG13/673, f. 26, p. 43, s. 277, 1901 England, Wales & Scotland Census; TNA, RG13/671, f. 107, p. 44, s. 315, 1901 England, Wales & Scotland Census.

49 *Surrey Comet*, 30 June 1900, p. 5.

50 TNA, HO107/1728, f. 308, p. 17, s. 74, 1851 England, Wales & Scotland Census; TNA RG09/894, f. 95, p. 19, s. 104 1861 England, Wales & Scotland Census; TNA RG10/1438, f. 96, p. 24, s. 113, 1871 England, Wales & Scotland Census.

51 *Oxford Chronicle*, 5 February 1876, p. 8.

52 Due to the prohibitive cost of divorce at this time, it is unsurprising to find that the working class who found themselves living in lodgings following marital breakdown were not legally separated.

53 *Nottingham Evening Post*, 1 August 1879, p. 3.

54 *Nottingham Evening Post*, 4 July 1882, p. 4.

55 *London Daily Chronicle*, 20 February 1858, p. 3.

56 We can trace Chadwick's early lodging years through his encounters with the Burnley court regarding the maintenance of his wife and family. *Burnley Express*, 17 May 1890, p. 7; *Burnley Express*, 14 June 1890, p. 6; *Burnley Express*, 20 September 1890, p. 6; Burnley Express, 11 October 1890, p. 7; *Burnley Express*, 25 July 1891, p. 6.

57 *Burnley Express*, 13 June 1894, p. 3.

58 *Oxford Times*, 17 February 1900, p. 8.

59 *Sunderland Daily Echo*, 20 August 1888, p. 3; *Sunderland Daily Echo*, 21 August 1888, p. 3

60 *Warwick and Warwickshire Advertiser*, 4 July 1840, p. 3.

61 *Kentish* Mercury, 11 May 1894, p. 3.

62 *Walthamstow and Leyton Guardian*, 6 July 1894, p. 3.

63 *London Evening Standard*, 23 June 1894, p. 1; July 1894, trial of JOHN GOLDIE ROUND (33) (t18940723–633), Old Bailey Proceedings Online, www.oldbaileyonline.org, version 8.0 (accessed 31 October 2023).

64 *Derbyshire Courier*, 15 July 1876, p. 7.

65 *Sheffield Evening Telegraph*, 30 January 1894, p. 3.

66 I have been unable to locate George Evans after he left his wife behind in Wadswick, so I cannot confirm his living arrangements after this point.

67 TNA, RG19, f. 133, p. 17, s. 131, 1891 England, Wales & Scotland Census; *Northampton Mercury*, 27 July 1900, p. 6.

68 For more information on the residential option of widowers and widowers see Vicky Holmes, *In Bed with the Victorians: The Life-Cycle of Working-Class Marriage* (Cham: Palgrave Macmillan), pp. 83–102.

69 TNA HO10/1522, f. 250, p. 5, s. 29, 1851 England, Wales & Scotland Census.

70 After the coroner's inquest and later poor law investigation in Hatfield's brother's death, Caroline Marks disappears from the record for over twenty years, when she then appears in Holborn Union Workhouse at the age of sixty-six. She died later that year. *Clerkenwell News*, 2 April 1870, p. 6; TNA, RG09/206, f. 88, p. 29, s. 183, 1861 England, Wales & Scotland Census; TNA RG12/247, f. 133, p. 9, s. 21, 1891 England, Wales & Scotland Census.

71 *Essex Standard*, 15 April 1864, p. 6. For information on this case, see Holmes, *In Bed with the Victorians*, pp. 91–5.

72 *Oxford Times*, 18 August 1900, p. 5.

73 *Essex Standard*, 15 April 1864, p. 6.

74 *Morning Herald* (London), 25 August 1840, p. 7.

75 TNA, RG09, 1161, f. 29, p. 21, s. 94, 1861 England, Wales & Scotland Census.

76 TNA RG09/878, f. 16, p. 26, s. 107, 1861 England, Wales & Scotland Census.

77 *Buckingham Advertiser*, 27 August 1870, p. 3.

78 *Ipswich Journal*, 8 February 1873, p. 8; TNA, RG10/1756, f.110, p. 10, 1871 England, Wales & Scotland Census.

3

The lodging exchange

In July 1900, a middle-aged man was unloading a wagon for his employer – farmer James Westwood of Belbroughton, Worcestershire – when he staggered and fell. Westwood promptly administered brandy, but 'the man' died soon after. The post-mortem identified sunstroke as the cause of death, but what the coroner's court could not determine was the identity of the man that lay before them. Seeking identification through Mrs Waldron, the woman with whom the stranger had recently taken lodgings in nearby Catshill, the coroner discovered 'She had not enquired his name, nor where he came from.'[1] Berating Waldron's foolishness in accepting a man into her home about whom she knew nothing 'led the coroner to remark on [her] excess of confidence in her fellow men, and to recommend her for her own sake to exercise more caution in taking in strange lodgers'.[2] The trope of the dark, shadowy stranger arriving at the door of an unsuspecting older woman lurks in the imagination. Just eleven years after Mrs Waldron's error, Marie Belloc Lowndes published *The Lodger* (1911), a story based on the Whitechapel murders of 1888, where Mrs Bunting and her husband unwittingly take in a strange lodger whom she later suspects to be the infamous killer. Such tropes continued throughout the first half of the twentieth century in both literature and film, culminating in the 1955 Ealing comedy *The Ladykillers*, where elderly widow Mrs Wilberforce becomes embroiled in a heist after the leader of a criminal gang takes lodgings in her lopsided home.[3] Yet the idea of the lodger as a stranger – dangerous or not – is a skewed one.

Challenging the idea of the lodger as a stranger in the home, Peter Baskerville's study of urban lodgers in the early-twentieth-century Canadian censuses contends that lodgers were not strangers but *familiar strangers*: not personally known to the accommodating householder but 'in the more general sense of class, religion, occupation, and ethnic background very familiar and not strange at all'.[4] More recently, however, historians have begun to suggest that lodgers may not have been strangers in any sense of the word. For example, Beatrice Moring has observed in Finnish oral history accounts of 'a system where the first lodgings of a young person from the countryside [to Helsinki] was with a relative or the relative of a neighbour from back home. Later lodgings were found through work mates.'[5] Meanwhile, Jeff Meek's study of boarding and lodging practices in early-twentieth-century Govan, Scotland, hints that among the familiar strangers, there were perhaps those even more closely connected to the household.[6] Finding connections across the censuses, Meek provides examples where, for instance, a person of the same surname as the householders is recorded in one census as a boarder and, in the next census, is revealed as a sibling. Notably, Meek does not rely on their shared surname to infer a kinship connection.[7] Shared surnames alone, after all, cannot be a clear indicator of familial relationships. As in the case of lodger Adam Robinson, whom we met in the previous chapter, he bore the same surname as the householder's married daughter, but as was made clear at the inquest: '[she is] no relation of mine'.[8] Meek also contests that connections were apparent between lodgers.[9] Indeed, as revealed below, Adam Robinson may not have been related to Mrs Allen's daughter, but he did have an existing relationship with another of the lodgers under Allen's roof.

Finding lodgings was just one part of the lodging exchange. Before crossing the threshold, the matter of what was to be provided and at what cost had to be negotiated between the householder and lodger. Locating such exchanges has long proved problematic, as the lodging contracts made among the working class were primarily verbal agreements.[10] However, this does not mean that the agreements between householders and lodgers are entirely absent from the record. Both Michael Anderson and Leonore Davidoff gathered a range of information about the monetary and services exchanges between householders and their lodgers from various sources, including reports of statistical societies, contemporary literature, and parliamentary papers. Such information not only revealed examples of how much was paid for lodgings but also details on what would be provided at varying costs, including beds, fire, lights, washing, and sundries.[11] Among these arrangements, Davidoff suggests what was provided was frequently distinguished along gender lines, with male lodgers tending to pay for board and other services more than their female counterparts.[12] Davidoff also hints that agreements surrounding the means of payment for lodgings might not have always been entirely monetary-based. Citing an enquiry by the Manchester Statistical Society in the 1860s, Davidoff states that 'about half the lodgers listed were not paying any rent'. Although she hedges, 'it is unclear whether they were kin or friends'.[13] More recently, Moring has noted the presence of such service exchanges in the lodging arrangement at the turn of the twentieth century in northern Europe, such as where 'female lodgers provided help in the household or male lodgers repaired shoes in return for having their clothes washed'.[14] Meanwhile, 'widows with young children seem to have ... taken in lodgers for the purpose of assistance with childcare'.[15]

This chapter, addressing some of the many questions regarding the lodging exchanges, looks to the inquest reports to provide answers through the lodgers' and householders' own accounts regarding their connections and agreements. The first section of this chapter, moving away from the Victorian census enumerators' interpretations, hears from lodgers and householders themselves about the connections between them. While I do not deny the presence of the stranger lodger in the home when – as was the case for Lowndes' fictional Buntings – no other lodgers or lodging could be found, most working-class householders and lodgers preferred not, in their close quarters, to live among strangers or, indeed, familiar strangers. Beyond the pages of fiction, migrants and non-migrants could find lodgings with workmates. At the same time, natives and established residents (those who had migrated and set up their own homes before coming to lodgings) could also turn to neighbours, friends, and even kin when they suddenly needed lodgings. Yet regardless of the connection, some form of agreement had to be made between the two parties as to what the lodging would comprise. Digging around the inquest reports, the second section of this chapter contributes to the discussion of 'what was provided' and at what cost. Highlighting the importance of the lodging exchange as a mutually beneficial arrangement, not just in terms of householders gaining income and lodgers affordable shelter, I unveil a level of flexibility in the lodging exchange and the importance of non-monetary exchanges between householders and their female lodgers.

Finding lodgings

Connections were at the core of the Victorian working-class lodgings exchange. Unlike Mrs Waldron, few thought it wise to accommodate a stranger under their roof, while lodgers themselves did not necessarily want to live with strangers. Even among the migrant lodger population, familiarity beyond the familiar stranger connection could be vital in obtaining domestic dwelling lodgings. Former acquaintances, for example, were called upon for lodgings after arriving in the area for work, especially among women for whom familiarity might add a certain level of security while away from home. When Charlotte Whale and Sarah Ellen Proctor, whom we met in Chapter 2, travelled from their native Staffordshire to Isleworth for the annual fruit picking, the two women did not lodge with strangers. Instead, they lodged with Ellen Callow, who 'said she knew [Whale] in Dudley' and that Whale had 'sent her a letter last week to say she was coming'.[16] Meanwhile, migrants with no one to call upon might first live in makeshift lodgings before forming connections in the workplace to more comfortable lodgings, as was the case for twenty-two-year-old George Bramley. In 1875, Bramley left his home in Bulwell, Nottinghamshire, and travelled to the Derbyshire colliery town of South Normanton to find employment in the pits, where, having first taken lodgings 'at the wooden huts', he then moved into the home of fellow colliery labourer William Starkey.[17] The presence of actual familiarity is not, however, to entirely discount the importance of the familiar stranger connections as stressed by Baskerville. When Irishman John Watson arrived in Derbyshire, he took employment at Staveley Company's farm iron works, where he also found lodgings with a fellow worker, Michael Welsh.[18] And, as the census the following year reveals, Welsh was also Irish, as was his wife and the four boarders that lodged under his roof on that particular night.[19]

The non-migrant population also found lodgings with workmates. But in contrast to the migrants searching for lodgings, non-migrants and established residents had probably not formed connections with workmates with the intention of finding lodgings. These lodgers, often initially secure in their home environments, were unlikely to be imagining a fall into lodgings when creating workmate connections. Instead, it had been the case that the workplace served as one of many spaces for the working class to foster a community that could provide connections to turn to in times of need, whatever that might be.[20] Nottingham framework knitter James Foster, whom we met in Chapter 2, had married, set up his own home, and grew a family. As he entered his forties, lodgings did not appear to be on the horizon. However, as seen, Foster was cast from the family home when his marriage deteriorated, and he found himself moving into lodgings just a short distance away in the home of a fellow framework knitter whom he had known for the past sixteen years.[21] And, when Ipswich native sixteen-year-old Emily Miller was forced from the family home due to overcrowding and 'Not lik[ing] to go to strangers', she found lodgings with a married woman she had worked with at a local clothing factory.[22] Yet the lodgings located via the workplace were not necessarily just with fellow workmates. In daily interactions with the women living in the vicinity, shop workers might have just as easily found lodgings over the counter with their regular customers. Adam Robinson and Robert Chadwick were employed at the greengrocers just '100 yards' from Mrs Mary Ann Allen's home. Chances are that they would have encountered Allen almost daily before lodging under her roof, as Robinson had done in the shop just hours before Allen's murder. Presumably, she had been collecting food for her lodgers' dinner.[23]

With walking the main means of travelling to and from work, natives and established residents generally found lodgings within a stone's throw of their workplace or former home. Our perpetual lodger from Chapter 2, John Hampson, took lodgings in the streets neighbouring the cotton mill where he worked most of his life. Indeed, many natives did not need to look further than a neighbouring house to find lodgings. As has been widely observed, alongside the small daily exchanges that existed among neighbours as part of everyday survival in working-class communities, there was a neighbourly obligation to assist during times of crisis, such as illness and eviction.[24] Accordingly, neighbours would be called upon for accommodation when the lodging necessity arose abruptly. On census night 1891, in the small iron mining community of Marton, Dalton in Furness, seventeen-year-old miner William Jackson was residing at home – No. 27 Marton – with his widowed mother and sibling. Just three years later, upon their mother's death, the family home was dismantled. Like the adolescent lodgers we met in Chapter 2, the Jackson children went in search of new accommodation. William, it seems, did not have to travel far, for an inquest held four months after his mother's death places him just a few doors away at No. 8 Marton.[25] Similarly, a coroner's inquest that same year just south of Marton in the cotton-weaving town of Burnley situates widower William Crossley living as a lodger with a former neighbour, in this case in the Lomas Street home of the above Mrs Mary Ann Allen, whose neighbour he had been when they both resided on Lydia Street during their respective marriages.[26] In some cases, the inquest reports yield direct examples of neighbourly requests for lodgings. When Elizabeth Houseley, wife of an engineman, was called before Chesterfield coroner's court to testify as to circumstances surrounding the death of waggon builder William Petheram, whose wife just weeks before had been committed to Mickleover asylum, she stated that Petheram 'lodged at our house. He was no relation of mine. [He had] lived next door to me. On being sold up he asked me to take him as a lodger, and I did so', even though they were well acquainted with his heavy drinking.[27]

Friends could also be turned to for lodgings. Of course, friendship is difficult to locate in the sources compared to the more tangible categories such as birthplace, workplace, neighbours, and kin. Moreover, as Carolyn Steedman and, more recently, Jamie L. Bronstein have observed, the term 'friend' among the nineteenth-century working class was sometimes used to describe a network of family members or simply patrons – such as friendly societies – called upon in times of economic distress, rather than companionate friendship. Nonetheless, as Bronstein argues, ties of actual friendship did exist among the working class.[28] Undoubtedly, friendship came into the equation in many of the above cases of lodgings found among workmates and neighbours. In some cases, however, the only connection that appears in the records is of friendship. For example, with a growing family and ill-health straining the household purse, the Cookes were forced to give up their home in their native Stroud. While they appear to have no kin with whom to find shelter, they did find lodgings that were not entirely unfamiliar a few streets away. As Eliza Cooke told the coroner's court investigating the death of their youngest child fifteen months after arriving at Mrs Richard's door in search of lodgings, she was 'an old friend of my mother's'.[29] Even in the supposed city of strangers, friends could provide lodgings at a moment's notice. Octogenarian Mary Corker, whom we met in the previous chapter, left her daughter's home – No. 2 Chesterfield Street, Marylebone – and, via the workhouse, arrived at No. 17 Pitt Street (now Scala Street), Tottenham Court Road, some thirty minutes walk away (though, given the noted decline in Mary's health, this may have taken somewhat longer) 'to lodge at the house of a friend'.[30]

Not only are friendship connections between householders and their lodgers evident in the inquest reports, but the inquest reports also reveal examples of ties of friendship between lodgers. Establishing the atmosphere in the Burnley home of Mrs Mary Ann Allen in the weeks leading up to her murder, the prosecution at the subsequent murder trial asked lodger Robert Chadwick – a man Crossley, Allen's paramour-lodger, believed was trying to take his place – 'Were you on friendly terms with Mrs Allen?' to which he responded 'We were all friends together.' Yet while this might not have been entirely the case, given the noted tensions in the house, at least one of Chadwick's friends lived under the same roof, for when lodger Adam Robinson took the stand at the criminal proceedings, he stated, 'he was a friend of Chadwick's'. Indeed, the two friends appear to have intentionally lodged together, moving into Allen's together just eight weeks before her murder and then, after her death, moving on to new lodgings together – having each given their address at the court proceedings as No. 98 Sandygate.[31] We also know that the two men had worked together at the same time in the grocer's shop that would have been frequented by Allen, though whether their friendship was formed in the workplace or elsewhere is not yielded in the records.[32] The inquest reports also reveal ties of friendship among the female lodger population. As noted above,

Charlotte Whale and Sarah Proctor annually travelled from their native Staffordshire to Isleworth in search of employment in the market garden, where the 'very good friends' – having grown up within a stone's throw of each other – took lodgings together and shared the same bed.[33]

The most familiar lodgers, however, were those lodging with kin. As noted above, the reliance on the census to unpick householder–lodger connections has undoubtedly left many kin-lodgers out in the cold. Of course, we could question whether kin can even be categorised as lodgers. Yet when we turn to the inquest reports, we find examples of clearly defined householder–lodger relationships between kin. As one sibling responded to a question posed by the coroner investigating her sister's death: 'Your sister is only a lodger with you? – That is all, sir.'[34] In the case of John Chesterman, married to the sister of the woman with whom he lodged, he found himself recorded in the inquest reports as both 'brother-in-law' and 'one of the lodgers'. Indeed, his own testimony confirms he lodged rather than lived with his sister-in-law: 'I have lodged here since last October.' However, Mercy Chesterman's relationship with the head of the household – her sister – is not entirely clear, for, given conventions at the time, she is defined only by her relationship with her husband.[35] Even when the census enumerator came knocking, some relatives were indefatigable when categorising the kin under their roof as lodgers. For example, tracing Robert Chadwick through the decades and establishing his family ties reveals that the married woman with whom he first lodged on his release from prison was Sarah Collinge, Robert's step-sister. Yet the relationship is not apparent in the 1891 census, for, with differing surnames and Chadwick listed only as their boarder, there is no hint whatsoever of a kinship connection.[36]

Siblings were not the only relatives turned to for lodgings. Extended family – nephews, nieces, cousins, and godparents – are all revealed in the inquest reports as providing lodging to kin. Such kinship appears to have been particularly important for those who had not begotten children to whom they would perhaps otherwise first turn for shelter. For example, forty-five-year-old bachelor wire bundler Richard Barrows 'lodged with his nephew' and, indeed, when we tie the name of the other lodger – McDonald – recorded in the inquest report to the census, we find that the nephew lodged not one but two bachelor uncles in his Warrington home.[37] Bachelor George Catchpool also turned to extended family for lodgings. As a soldier and a policeman, Catchpool had 'been about the world a great deal', but as time passed and old age set in, the wandering Catchpool returned to his native Suffolk, where – evidently having not lost his kinship connections during his travels – he went to live with his niece 'as a lodger'.[38] More grounded in a sense of place, Cheshire spinster Betsy Heald had spent much of her adult life living with close kin, first her father and then her sister. However, when her sister died, Betsy was left without a home.[39] Whether she first turned to her brother, greengrocer Thomas Heald, living nearby on Crown Street, for shelter, we do not know. It is possible, given his testimony at the inquest into her death, that he might well have turned away his sister on account of her 'addict[ion] to drink', as seen in Chapter 2 with the son of Owen Girdlestone turning out his father on account of his drinking.[40] Nevertheless, there was alternative kin she could turn to for lodgings: her cousin, James Deakin, on Church Street, where he and his wife already accommodated numerous lodgers. Yet when we dig deeper into the connections between extended kin in the householder–lodger relationship, it becomes apparent they had been turned to in some cases because of a closer intimacy. Betsy Heald, the newspaper reporting on her death reveals, was 'on terms of intimacy with the [Deakin] family', so for her, her cousin might well have been the obvious choice for lodgings following her sister's death.[41] And when Huddersfield cotton spinner Joseph Pogson went in search of lodgings following the death of his wife, he went to live as a paying lodger with his married niece whom – as the inquest report details – 'he brought up from a child'.[42]

However, the presence of 'intimate' kin-lodgers was not without its tensions. Margaret Deakin, James Deakin's wife, was noted to quarrel with Betsy, even at times coming to blows before finally murdering her as she lay on the bed in the room that they shared. And, while Joseph Pogson had appeared to live amicably with his niece and her husband, Joseph Haigh, for twelve years, as Haigh began to suffer from delusions, the relationship deteriorated: 'They have not been on good terms. I believe [Haigh] wanted the deceased to leave. He did not do.'[43] Given such tensions, we have to ask whether taking in a kin-lodger was, like neighbours, born from a sense of obligation or whether it was the case that their fellow kin could not manage without taking them as lodgers. For example, we cannot be sure whether Mary Burdock (née Sloper, Webb) was pleased about lodging her married sister and husband under her roof. Indeed, as a newspaper report entitled 'Unfriendly Sisters' revealed, the year after the inquest into Mary's husband's death that placed her sister and brother-in-law as lodgers in her home, the Chestermans had moved on. In the report, tensions between the sisters are revealed, for Mercy, now of 46 Friar Street, stood charged before the City Court 'for damaging a jacket to the extent of 8s., the property of her sister, Mary Burdock, 5, Bridewell Square'.[44] We know from Chapter 1 that Mary could not maintain her home without the income from lodgers due to her husband's lack of contribution to the household. Had it then been the case of 'better the devil you know?' Meanwhile, in perhaps one of the less conventional setups, Cumberland farm labourer Jacob Skelton had taken his elderly father-in-law, farmer Robert Irwin, as a lodger, seemingly not because of cordial relations but because he could not financially maintain his home without him. He 'was a lodger with us, and paid us 5s. a week ... Seven was the bargain, but there was two to remain on for the house rent and the likes of that in case we stood need of it.'[45] In other words, as referred to in another inquest report, there was an 'understanding that he was to give the 2s. a week more if they were back on their rent'.[46] Yet Skelton and his father-in-law had a complex, challenging, and, on occasion, violent relationship. Just before his death (for which Skelton was arrested and then later acquitted), Irwin had expressed to neighbours his unhappiness in his living situation and thus became set on finding new lodgings. He never did, and his death resolved the Skelton's financial struggles, for while Irwin had provided a financial buffer in life, Jacob Skelton received a 'windfall' – as the *Carlisle Journal* referred to it – upon Irwin's death. Irwin had saved a considerable sum of money during his life, which he bequeathed to his daughter. But with this inheritance received before 1870 – the year that began successive married women's property acts – the money, all £200, became her husband's property. From this point, the Skeltons would never need to worry about making the weekly rent again.[47]

Monetary matters

Before taking a place in the home, the lodger had to agree to the rent and other charges that would be part of their lodging arrangement. Lodgings were generally paid weekly, with most domestic dwelling lodgers, unlike Irwin, paying between one and two shillings a week for their lodgings and additional sums for board and other services. As observed in Chapter 1, the payment from one lodger covered around one-third of the householder's weekly rent. However, the cost of lodgings could be up for negotiation. Juxtaposed with Irwin's expandable rent, some impoverished female lodgers – in what appears to be a kindness – found their rent reduced. For example, Catherine McDonough 'usually charge[d] one shilling and sixpence' for lodgings in her home, No. 8 Ludgate Street, Manchester, but when a destitute orange and apple seller, fifty-five-year-old Mary Hunter, arrived at her home searching for lodgings, McDonough charged her just 'eight pence a week'. McDonough's explanation for the reduced lodging charge when testifying at the coroner's court investigating Mary Hunter's death was: 'I took her [in] for the sake of company, because she was religious, and I liked her for what she said to me.'[48]

But what did the lodger expect for their money? Except for those homes where the family did not have a recognisable bed on which to sleep, lodgers were typically supplied with a bed and bedding. However, while generally at the higher end of the payment scale and where space permitted, a lodger might be fortunate enough to have a room of their own, most lodgers – in the cramped space that was the working-class home – would, as we shall see in the next chapter, share a bedroom or, indeed, a bed with other lodgers or, on occasion, family members. Those paying solely for lodgings – whom the GRO refer to as lodgers – might have the use of the fire to prepare their own meals or choose to eat them elsewhere. Except, that is perhaps on Sundays. As Beatrice Moring found in 1900 Finland, 'If the lodger was not also boarding ... dinner on Sunday [was] usually included in the rent.'[49] Receiving Sunday dinner as part of his lodging charge appears to have been the case for George Henry Day, who lodged in the Southampton home of a couple named Berry: 'I boarded myself', but on Sunday (at least on the Sunday Mrs Berry was murdered) '[Mrs Berry] got my dinner.'[50] Those who wanted food 'got' for them on other days of the week would have had to pay extra.

Though lodgers tended to refer to themselves as 'lodgers', as did the householders, many of the men living in working-class homes also boarded. It is not always possible to work out how much was paid for board on top of lodgings as the amount detailed in the inquest reports was generally totalled, but there are occasional cases where the charge was stated or could, at least, be worked out. Those who boarded paid as little as 3s. 6d. a week for board and lodgings, although some householders charged as much as 7s. 8d. a week for board.[51] Widow Ann Dawson, for example, had two lodgers: 'One pays 10s. per week for board and lodging, and the other 2s. 4d. per week, but he had no board.'[52] While few inquest reports hint at the food prepared for the lodgers – with occasional mention of meat, bacon, and potatoes – they reveal that those lodgers who boarded could expect breakfast, dinner, and an evening meal. Frederick Joseph Royals, a clerk at the Ashbourne Brewery, lodging in the home of a widow in her fifties, Mrs Mary Allen (not to be confused with Mrs Mary Ann Allen), certainly expected to arrive at the table with meals ready for him.[53] Returning home at 10.30 one evening, he was surprised to find Allen had gone to bed 'but had not prepared his supper, which was unusual'. The following morning, rising about eight o'clock, discovered 'His breakfast was not ready, and the fire was not lighted. Thinking it strange, he went upstairs, and knocked at [Allen's] door, but got no answer.' Royals finally raised the alarm after getting ready for work and knocking again. A neighbour, breaking into her room, found her dead. It was concluded she had been dead for some time.[54] Male lodgers who boarded also joined the dinnertime departure from the workplace. Mrs Mary Ann Allen's lodgers, who lodged and boarded at the cost of 3s. 6d. a week and, as noted earlier, worked just a stone's throw away from their lodgings, returned at noon each working day to find a cooked meal ready at the kitchen table. Not everyone, however, could return for their meals during the day. In such instances, provisions were prepared to be taken by or delivered to the lodger who boarded. For example, before he departed for work at the Woolwich Arsenal at half-past five, forty-year-old labourer Charles Hughes was 'handed ... his breakfast tied in a handkerchief' by labourer Michael Barry, the married man with whom Hughes lodged.[55] And, just before noon on Friday in August 1888, Mrs Ellis's twelve-year-old daughter set out from home with a 'basin tied in a handkerchief … and a bottle of milk' and headed along the towpath to the Northwich Vale Royal to deliver dinner to their lodger, brick setter's labourer Enoch Appleton.[56]

In addition to board and lodgings, lodgers could also pay for attendance. 'Attendance', Leonore Davidoff concludes from a reading of Charles Munby's diaries, including 'cleaning, carrying water and coal, emptying slops … and chamber pots, making fires, running errands (with a kiss on the stairs if the lodgers could snatch it)' – the latter being a matter I return to in Chapter 5.[57] In mentions of attendance on a lodger in the inquest reports, unsurprisingly, the lodger was typically male, with several inquest reports referring to female householders discovering the bodies of their male lodgers when entering to clean their lodger's sleeping quarters. Female lodgers, it seems, were expected to attend to themselves. Questioned as to how her lodger, Deborah Willis, could have lived in such squalor – '[her] room was in a filthy state' – Julia Toler replied that she 'used to keep the room as clean as [she] could', but it was Willis's 'duty to keep it clean'.[58] The men who did attend to themselves appear to have done so out of personal preference rather than an expectation that they would do so themselves, such as seventy-one-year-old mason Samuel May who, when it came to his lodging room, 'did all the necessary work himself'.[59]

An extra charge would also be added for washing and mending clothes. As board and attendance were not necessarily mutually inclusive, we can find some evidence surrounding the charge for attendance and other services. We do not know why John Last boarded himself in the Vincents' Ipswich home, but we do know he paid 2s. 6d. a week for his lodgings, along with 'washing and mending and seeing after him'. Subtracting the cost of less-than-comfortable lodgings, at around 1s. to 1s. 6d. a day, Last's washing, mending, and attendance would have amounted to around 2d. a day. Yet Last's case also highlights that attendance could vary from household to household. When he died from pneumonia under the Vincents' roof – the home he had lodged in for fourteen years – what 'seeing after him' actually entailed came under intense scrutiny by the investigating coroner, questioning whether, in not caring for her sick lodger, Mrs Vincent had been guilty of neglecting the duties Last had paid for. Guiding the jury, the coroner stated the jury needed to determine whether Mrs Vincent was in some way responsible for Last's death, and therefore, 'they might have to consider ... what was included in the undertaking of seeing after the deceased'. However, with no clear legal definition of what constituted attendance, it was difficult to determine responsibility. In the end, the jury found that Mrs Vincent's action or rather inaction had accelerated her lodger's death, but – erring on the sympathetic side as juries tended to do – they believed the neglect resulted from ignorance rather than malice, and thus Vincent was not legally responsible. Nonetheless, they concluded that as he 'had lived at the house so many years, he should have been looked after'.[60]

Female householders sometimes also provide childcare for a fee for those lodgers with children as part of the lodging arrangement, an arrangement that thus enabled parents to go out to work without the need to find childcare beyond their lodgings. For example, the Deakins, as well as taking in numerous lodgers into their Cheshire home, also provided childcare at a charge for at least one of their lodgers, although the task was farmed off to another of their lodgers.[61] Yet while we might assume that all those lodgers seeking childcare were female, the inquest reports suggest that the domestic dwelling lodging arrangement also provided lone men with dependent children the childcare they needed to retain their work. As I have shown elsewhere and below, some men – either martially separated or widowed – might take in a female lodger to provide duties that would have otherwise been their wives', including childcare.[62] However, when he took custody of his children, Robert Chadwick, already living as a lodger, paid Mrs Mary Ann Allen 10s. a week on top of his board and lodgings for her to care for and feed his children. Notably, this was the exact amount he repeatedly denied his estranged wife for maintenance, claiming to the courts that he did not earn enough money to pay for such an amount.[63]

Working-class householders sometimes offered to lodge the sick in their homes for an additional charge. Before changes under the New Poor Law, boarding out sick paupers had been a common practice of the authorities.[64] While such a practice dwindled in the Victorian era with the rise of the institution, as my work has shown elsewhere, families not wishing to commit relatives to the horror of workhouse or asylum sought lodgings for their ailing relatives.[65]

As seen in Chapter 2, in the mid-1840s, hairdresser George Evans, with his wife's declining health – she was described in the newspaper as a 'paralytic [and] subject to a deranged state of mind' – returned to her native Wiltshire and found her lodgings in the home of labourer Thomas Jordan and his wife, paying 10s. a week for her lodgings, board, and care. Afterwards, he headed to London, presumably searching for employment and lodgings for himself. Yet while undoubtedly many ailing lodgers were well cared for, without regulation – such as was the case with baby farming in the early part of the Victorian period – these arrangements could tip into neglect. When George Evans could no longer meet the payments due to his own ill health, the Jordans ceased caring for Martha. When Martha died under their roof, an inquest was promptly opened. One witness, a neighbour, widow Mary Munford, told the coroner's court she had heard several blows and Mrs Jordan swearing at Martha. The medical witness, however, could not find any signs of violence upon her body. Nonetheless, she 'was emaciated [and] there had been much disease, so as to require medical and surgical treatment', for the Jordans had not sought medical treatment for Martha, nor had they been feeding her. Unsurprisingly then, the jury concluded that while her death was from natural causes, they were 'of the opinion that death was accelerated from want of medical assistance, and they regret that the parties with whom she lodged had not applied for the same'.[66]

We would perhaps expect rent arrears to be more easily collected when the lodger under the roof was the one responsible for payment. Of course, most lodgers – those more silent in the records – paid their dues each week, accruing perhaps occasional arrears that were promptly addressed. However, on occasion, working-class householders would face the problem of lodgers who *could not* or *would not* pay. The first recourse for householders was to politely and regularly remind lodgers of money owed. For example, when Slough blacksmith Frederick Moody and his wife Sarah Ann took their neighbour's twenty-three-year-old son, gravel-getter William Alfred James, as their lodger, they soon found him an unreliable source of income. Sarah Ann got 'in the habit of asking him for his rent', but within two months, James was in arrears amounting to 6s. 6d. Despite asking morning and night 'for her money', Sarah Ann received only 1s. 6d. Before the remaining amount could be collected, James was arrested for a murder that had taken place in the town. Whether James settled the debt after his acquittal two months later, we do not know. Perhaps, to redeem what was owed, the Moodys sold whatever possessions James had left under their roof.[67]

Householders had the same rights as landlords regarding their lodgers' arrears. The 'Distress for Rent' Act, passed in 1737, allowed householders to detain and sell their lodger's goods in place of unpaid rent. Although given the complexities in collecting distress for rent, how often these rights were exercised is subject to speculation. Obtaining what was owed had to adhere to a strict protocol: lodgers had to be in arrears, certain items (such as a tradesman's tools) could not be detained, distress could not be made after dark, householders were required to make an inventory and provide a copy to the lodger, and no less than five days must have elapsed before the detained property could be sold but not before being appraised by two sworn brokers.[68] Failure to do any of the above could result in lodgers taking legal proceedings, which is precisely what happened to London shoemaker forty-six-year-old Henry John Battersbee. When we first meet Battersbee in Chapter 1, he had taken a lodger to alleviate his family's struggle. Yet instead, the lodger merely added to Battersbee's woes, as he was not always forthcoming with their weekly rent payment. Therefore, Battersbee decided to take matters into his own hands and 'sold some goods of a lodger for rent due'. However, in doing so, he broke the law. Battersbee had not only sold his lodger's property for 'rent due' rather than arrears but had done so without the assistance of a sworn broker. Unsurprisingly then, the lodger – clearly understanding their rights as a lodger – threatened legal proceedings against Battersbee. However, this particular matter of arrears ended up in a very different court, namely the coroner's court, with the threat proving to be the final straw that drove Battersbee to suicide.[69]

Domestic currencies

All the above assumes that the lodging exchange was always a direct exchange of money for services. However, this was far from the case among the lodging exchanges between women, who, when necessary, would barter with informal currencies to find a bed. As explored in Chapter 1, female lodgers providing childcare facilitated the means for wives and mothers to seek paid work outside the home. In turn, they would receive free or reduced lodgings. This number was by no means insignificant in some areas of the country. As Henry Carne Oats found for the Manchester districts of Deansgate and Ancoats in the 1860s, of lodgers who did not pay any rent – who in an area of Deansgate amounted to 285 out of 511 lodgers – many '[took] care of the house or the children as an equivalent for their lodgings'.[70] Keeping house and undertaking childcare in exchange for lodgings appears to be the predominant informal currency in the lodging market, albeit sometimes extending to supporting the householder's wider economic needs. When elderly spinster Betsy Heald took up lodgings with the Deakins, she had little means to pay for weekly lodgings. Instead, they struck a deal where Betsy would pay 'only a small sum for her lodgings' and, in exchange, assist in the Deakin's provision shop and take charge of the other lodgers' children.[71]

Companionship appears to have also played a secondary, if not a primary, role in negotiating such an arrangement. Separating from her second husband, forty-year-old Ann Dagan and her daughter went in search of lodgings. Such was their dire situation – with Ann out of work and her daughter, a factory worker, earning a wage of just 5s. 6d. – the two women could not hope to afford domestic dwelling lodgings. Instead, they arrived at the door of Mary Battle's (unregistered) lodging house on East Albert Street, Spedding's Fold, Barnsley, hoping to exchange work for cheap lodgings. Fortune appeared to be on their side. Seeing an opportunity to console her recently widowed daughter through female companionship, Battle agreed that the two women could lodge at her daughter's house in exchange for Ann doing her work – cooking meals, making beds, etc. – in the lodging house. And, on the days Ann worked, she would, in return, receive her meals.[72]

Female lodgers also used their domestic skills to negotiate lodgings with those men lacking spouses. As with the lone male lodger, the question of who would 'do' for him also applied to male-headed householders living alone through separation or bereavement. In a case I discuss elsewhere, for example, poverty-stricken Adelaide Peters left her husband behind in the workhouse and went in search of work and shelter, finding both with Walter Stammers, a man separated from his wife, who offered Peters 'board and lodging in consideration of her keeping his children'.[73] In similar straitened circumstances, elderly widow Jane Mizen found lodgings with forty-six-year-old relieving officer and widower Edmund Parsons in exchange for housekeeping and the charge of his daughter.[74]

Conclusion

This chapter has moved beyond the idea of the lodgers as strangers. Although I do not deny the presence of such lodgers in the Victorian working-class home when needs must – Mrs Waldron must have been in dire straits to take in an unknown lodger without asking any questions as to his identity – many of the migrants and non-migrants identified in the inquest reports relied on those familiar to them within their various networks for lodgings. Both near and far, workmates, neighbours, and friends provided accommodation to those searching for lodgings. Indeed, the inquest reports reveal that such networks also extended to blood ties by bringing the kin-lodger to the table. Whether those familiar – kin and non-kin – accommodated those in their networks as lodgers out of obligation, necessity, or compassion is not always clear from the inquest reports. What is clear, however, from the inquest reports is that familiar or not, some form of a lodging contract was generally negotiated between the two parties as to what would be paid by the lodger and what they would receive in return from the householder.

Many domestic dwelling lodgers, such as those who sat around Mrs Mary Ann Allen's table on the day of her murder, paid not only for their bed but also for board and attendance. However, confirming Davidoff's suggestion, the lodging exchanges revealed in the inquest reports were decidedly gendered. Men tended to pay for board and services to ensure all their domestic needs were met by the female householder. In contrast, female lodgers were expected to be able to see to themselves domestically, as well as provide assistance around the home. Yet as the inquest reports also reveal, this domestic delineation saw, in some cases, payment for lodgings itself drawn along gendered lines. In a world where informal economies still played a vital role in daily survival among the working class, especially among women, we see that while wage-earning men tended to pay for their lodgings with money, women with little monetary means could negotiate and exchange domestic assistance for lodgings. Such non-monetary exchanges for lodgings, however, as we have seen, tended to be mutually beneficial arrangements with the householders often requiring what the lodger had to offer.

Finally, as hinted at in this chapter, in the working-class home, lodgers did not live separately from the householders with whom they lodged. Instead, as I discuss in the next chapter, their daily lives appear entirely entwined. Having established the connections between lodgers and householders and brought the agreements between them to the fore, we now move on to explore the practicalities of that arrangement between lodgers and householders, from eating to sleeping and the daily social interactions, both at times of concord and conflict.

Notes

1 Several Mrs Waldrons were living in Catshill at this time; therefore, with the inquest report omitting her forename, it is impossible to determine which Mrs Waldron had taken in the unfamiliar lodger.

2 Questioning of witnesses suggests that the man may have been recently widowed and survived by several children. However, it was not until a notebook of the deceased had been found that they came any closer to identifying him. The notebook contained: 'The recurrence of the name James Smith [which] pointed to this being the name of the deceased and that he came from Manchester … it appeared [he] had knowledge of shorthand, and from some entries in the book it could be traced that [he] had been a canvasser for the Liverpool Victoria Friendly Society.' However, neither the police nor the coroner were able to verify this information. *Bromsgrove & Droitwich Messenger*, 21 July 1900, p. 6.

3 For an in-depth discussion of the representation of lodgers in literature and film, see Chiara Briganti and Kathy Mezei (eds), *Living with Strangers: Bedsits and Boarding Houses in Modern English Life, Literature and Film* (London: Bloomsbury, 2018).

4 Peter Baskerville, 'Familiar Strangers: Urban Families with Boarders, Canada, 1901', *Social Science History*, 25:3 (2001), 322–3. DOI: 10.1017/S0145553200012141.

5 Beatrice Moring, 'Women, Work and Survival Strategies in Urban Northern Europe Before the First World War', in Beatrice Moring (ed.), *Female Economic Strategies in the Modern World* (London: Routledge, 2012), p. 61.

6 Jeff Meek, 'Boarding and Lodging Practices in Early Twentieth-Century Scotland', *Continuity and Change*, 31:1 (2016), 81–92. DOI: 10.1017/S0268416016000084. Similarly, Di Cooper and Moira Donald have shown in the case of servant–householder relationships that a person might bear 'a different surname from the head of the household, and yet found to be related to the family'. Di Cooper and Moira Donald, 'Households and "Hidden" Kin in Early-Nineteenth-Century England: Four Case Studies in Suburban Exeter, 1821–1861', *Continuity and Change*, 10:2 (1995), 262. DOI: 10.1017/S026841600000268X.

7 Meek, 'Boarding and Lodging', 81–92.

8 *Burnley Gazette*, 16 June 1894, p. 8.

9 Meek, 'Boarding and Lodging', 88.

10 Joanne McEwan concludes that a written legal contract would have unlikely formed part of the lodging arrangements among the poor and working classes. Joanne McEwan, 'The Lodging Exchange: Space, Authority and Knowledge in Eighteenth-Century London', in Joanne McEwan and Pamela Sharpe (eds), *Accommodating Poverty: The Housing and Living Arrangements of the English Poor, c.1600–1850* (London: Palgrave Macmillan, 2011), pp. 55–6.

11 Michael Anderson found that in mid-nineteenth-century Manchester, 9d. to 1s. 3d. would provide a place in the family's bedroom, 'benefitting from their fire and lights', whereas 1s. to 1s. 6d. a week would get the lodger a single unfurnished room, coal, and candles, and, 'for another few pence', washing materials and sundries. And, in nearby Preston, 1s. to 2s. 6d. a week would also get the lodger a place at the family table, albeit providing their own food to be cooked by the landlady. Michael Anderson, *Family Structure in Nineteenth Century Lancashire* (Cambridge: Cambridge University Press, 1971), p. 47.

12 Leonore Davidoff, 'The Separation of Home and Work? Landladies and Lodgers in Nineteenth-and Twentieth-Century England', in Sandra Burman (ed.), *Fit Work for Women* (London: Croom Helm, 1979), p. 82.

13 Leonore Davidoff, Megan Doolittle, Janet Fink, and Katherine Holden, *The Family Story: Blood, Contract, and Intimacy, 1830–1960* (London: Longman, 1999), p. 179. There were at least two enquiries undertaken by Henry Carnes Oats on behalf of the Manchester Statistical Society on the living conditions of certain districts of Manchester that included statistical detail on the accommodation of lodgers in domestic

dwellings. Manchester Statistical Society, *Inquiry into the educational and other conditions of a district of Deansgate* (Manchester, 1864), pp. 6, 12; Manchester Statistical Society, *Inquiry into the educational and other conditions of a district in Ancoats* (Manchester, 1865), pp. 10, 16.

14 Moring, 'Women, Work and Survival Strategies', p. 62.

15 Beatrice Moring, 'Widows, Children and Assistance from Society in Urban Northern Europe 1890–1910', *The History of the Family*, 13:1 (2008), 110. DOI: 10.1016/j.hisfam.2008.01.005.

16 *Isleworth Echo* (London), 20 April 1888, p. 4.

17 *Derbyshire Courier*, 5 February 1876, p. 8.

18 *Derbyshire Courier*, June 23, 1870, p. 3.

19 TNA, RG10/3622, f. 26, p. 2, s. 14, 1871 England, Wales & Scotland Census.

20 Richard Dennis and Stephen Daniels, '"Community" and the Social Geography of Victorian Cities', *Urban History*, 8 (1981), 14. DOI: 10.1017/S0963926800005265.

21 *Nottingham Evening Post*, 4 July 1882, p. 4.

22 *Ipswich Journal*, 23 November 1867, p. 5. For more information on this case, see Vicky Holmes, 'Accommodating the Lodger: The Domestic Arrangements of Lodgers in Working-Class Dwellings in a Victorian Provincial Town', *Journal of Victorian Culture*, 19:3 (2014), 314–31. DOI: 10.1080/13555502.2014.947181.

23 *Burnley Express*, 14 July 1894, p. 8.

24 As Ellen Ross observed, 'In emergencies like serious illness or an eviction, neighbours could be counted on for major services, something not contingent on having maintained cordial ties, but on the obligations that people viewed as part of "the neighbour role" ... Evicted families would be taken in. An observer of a 1905 winter demolition project in East London which required the removal of several households wrote: "Before the day was out, every one of the twenty or so inhabitants had been taken in by neighbours as poor and crowded as themselves."' Ellen Ross, 'Survival Networks: Women's Neighbourhood Sharing in London Before World War I', *History Workshop Journal*, 15:1 (1983), 6. DOI: 10.1093/hwj/15.1.4.

25 TNA, RG12/3478, f. 34, p. 8, s. 47, 1891 England, Wales & Scotland Census; *Soulby's Ulverston Advertiser and General Intelligencer*, 30 November 1893, p. 5 – their mother, fifty-eight-year-old Margaret Jackson, died on 23 November 1893. *Soulby's Ulverston Advertiser and General Intelligencer*, 22 March 1894, p. 7.

26 We know that Allen was a resident at no. 4. Lydia Street – in a neighbouring house to Crossley and his new wife – in the latter part of 1891, for she was advertising for 'washing wanted' at that address. *Burnley*

Express, 14 November 1891, p. 4. Just the week before the advertisement had been placed by Allen, Crossley had married widow Sarah Bowes, both giving their address as Lydia Street.

27 *Derbyshire Courier*, 15 July 1876, p. 6.

28 Jamie L. Bronstein, *The Happiness of the British Working Class* (Redwood City, CA: Stanford University Press, 2023), pp. 78–81; Carolyn Steedman, *An Everyday Life of the English Working Class: Work, Self and Sociability in the Early Nineteenth Century* (Cambridge: Cambridge University Press, 2013), pp. 54–78.

29 Edwin Cooke, a sticker worker, and his wife Eliza had, on the night of the 1891 census, been residing in their own home of Middle Hill. TNA, RG12/2024, f. 103, p. 13, s. 83, 1891 England, Wales & Scotland Census; *Stroud Journal*, 28 December 1894, p. 5.

30 *Morning Herald* (London), 25 August 1840, p. 7.

31 *Burnley* Express, 4 July 1894, p. 3.

32 *Burnley Express*, 11 October 1890, p. 7; TNA, RG12/3367, f. 115, p. 7, s. 47, 1891 England, Wales & Scotland Census.

33 *Middlesex Independent*, 21 April 1888, p. 3.

34 *Hull Packet*, 22 September 1882, p. 7; *Eastern Morning News*, 18 September 1882, p. 3.

35 *Oxfordshire Weekly News*, 15 August 1888, p. 2.

36 TNA, RG12/3365, f. 117, p. 62, s. 350, 1891 England, Wales & Scotland Census. A newspaper report regarding Chadwick's ongoing maintenance cases identifies Mrs Collinge as 'Chadwick's sister'. *Burnley Express*, 11 October 1890, p. 7.

37 *Runcorn Advertiser*, 23 February 1900, p. 6. McDonald is listed in the 1901 census, in terms of his relationship to the head of household, as 'Uncle'. The inquest report, however, refers to him as a lodger. TNA RG13/3581, f. 7, p. 6, s. 26, 1901 England, Wales & Scotland Census.

38 *Ipswich Journal*, 29 February 1876, p. 2.

39 Betsy Heald had been living with her father on the night of the 1861 census. However, by 1871, she was living with her sister – a shopkeeper – on Tabley Street, where, as the census suggests, she remained for at least ten years. TNA, RG09/2604, f. 48, p. 35, s. 192, 1861 England, Wales & Scotland Census; TNA, RG10/3697, f. 110, p. 4, s. 17, 1871 England, Wales & Scotland Census; TNA, RG11/ 3526, f. 69A, p. 30, s. 609, 1881 England, Wales & Scotland Census.

40 *Cheshire Observer*, 3 February 1894, p. 6; *Chester Courant*, 27 June 1894, p. 6. Thomas Heald was residing on nearby Crown Street on the night of the 1891 census. TNA, RG12/2838, f. 132, p. 23, s. 125, 1891 England, Wales & Scotland Census.

41 *Cheshire Observer*, 3 February 1894, p. 6; *Chester Courant*, 27 June 1894, p. 6; *Runcorn Guardian*, 31 January 1894, p. 5.
42 *Huddersfield Chronicle*, 14 May 1864, p. 7. Notably, there is no record of the lodging relationship in either census when Joseph resided with his niece. In 1851, he was recorded as a visitor, then ten years later as 'uncle'. TNA, HO107/2295, f. 848, p. 32, s. 121, 1851 England, Wales & Scotland Census; RG09/3268, f. 80, p. 19, s. 98, 1861 England, Wales & Scotland Census.
43 *Huddersfield Chronicle*, 14 May 1864, p. 7.
44 *Oxford Chronicle*, 17 August 1889, p. 8.
45 *Carlisle Journal*, 8 January 1858, p. 8.
46 *Carlisle Journal*, 26 February 1858, p. 7.
47 Following Irwin's death, the Skeltons moved to South Shields, Durham, where Jacob was employed as a brickyard labourer. Thereafter, the family have so far been untraceable in the census. TNA, RG09/3795, f. 58, p. 15, s. 62, 1861 England, Wales & Scotland Census.
48 *Northern Star*, 5 January 1850, p. 6; *Manchester Times*, 2 January 1850, p. 5.
49 Beatrice Moring, 'Gender, Class and Lodging in Urban Finland Around 1900', *Continuity and Change*, 31:1 (2016), 57. DOI: 10.1017/S0268416016000102.
50 *Hampshire Advertiser*, 3 January 1900, p. 3.
51 For example, Julia Toler, in 1860s Colchester, charged her female lodger – Deborah Willis – just 6d. a day for food. *Essex Standard*, 15 April 1864, p. 6. For more details on this case, see Vicky Holmes, *In Bed with the Victorians: The Life-Cycle of Working-Class Marriage* (Cham: Palgrave Macmillan, 2017), pp. 91–5.
52 *Norfolk News*, 17 March 1900, p. 3.
53 TNA, RG12/2753, f. 63, p. 3, s. 17, 1891 England, Wales & Scotland Census.
54 *Derbyshire Advertiser and Journal*, 1 December 1894, p. 6; *Ashbourne News Telegraph*, 30 November 1894, p. 4.
55 *Woolwich Gazette*, 21 December 1888, p. 2.
56 *Northwich Guardian*, 4 August 1888, p. 4.
57 Davidoff, 'The Separation of Home and Work', p. 82.
58 *Essex Standard*, 15 April 1864, p. 6.
59 *Islington Gazette*, 2 February 1888, p. 2.
60 *Ipswich Journal*, 6 January 1894, p. 2.
61 *Chester Courant*, 27 June 1894, p. 6: *Chester Courant*, 31 January 1894, p. 5; *Crewe Guardian*, 31 January 1894, p. 5; *Crewe Guardian*, 10 February 1894, p. 2.
62 Holmes, *In Bed with the Victorians*, p. 71.

63 *Burnley Express*, 17 May 1890, p. 7; *Burnley Express*, 14 June 1890, p. 6; *Burnley Express*, 20 September 1890, p. 6; *Burnley Express*, 11 October 1890, p. 7; *Burnley Express*, 25 July 1891, p. 6; *Burnley Express*, 14 July 1894, p. 8.

64 For more details on this practice, see Steven King, *Sickness, Medical Welfare and the English Poor, 1750–1834* (Manchester: Manchester University Press, 2018). Laurel Daen's work on the sick and the disabled in eighteenth-century Massachusetts has also demonstrated the commonality of paupers with physical and intellectual disabilities, as well as the elderly, being boarded out by the state, often to households that required additional income. Daen also illustrates that such an arrangement could burden the household, particularly the women who had to provide round-the-clock care and nursing. Laurel Daen, '"To Board & Nurse a Stranger": Poverty, Disability, and Community in Eighteenth-Century Massachusetts', *Journal of Social History*, 53:3 (2020), 716–41. DOI: 10.1093/jsh/shy117.

65 Vicky Holmes, 'Accommodating the Lodger', 328–30.

66 *Wilts and Gloucestershire Standard*, 8 September 1846, p. 3.

67 Also known as Bill Atkins. *Reading Mercury*, 29 December 1888, p. 2; *Maidenhead Advertiser*, 2 January 1889, p. 4.

68 John Mayhall, *A Plain Guide to Landlords Tenants and Lodgers with a Collection of Useful Forms*, 3rd edition (London, 1862), pp. 12–22. Also see Samuel Orchard, *Beeton's Law Book: A Practical Compendium of the General Principles of English Jurisprudence* (London: Ward Lock and Tyler, 1876), pp. 410–13.

69 *Morning Post*, 5 November 1846, p. 6.

70 Manchester Statistical Society, *Inquiry into the Educational and Other Conditions of a District of Deansgate* (Manchester, 1864), pp. 6, 12; Manchester Statistical Society, *Inquiry into the Educational and Other Conditions of a District in Ancoats* (Manchester, 1865), pp. 10, 16.

71 *Chester Courant*, 27 June 1894, p. 6: *Chester Courant*, 31 January 1894, p. 5; *Crewe Guardian*, 31 January 1894, p. 5; *Crewe Guardian*, 10 February 1894, p. 2.

72 Mary Malin (née Battle) had only just lost her husband, Henry Malin, aged twenty-two years, in the Swaite Main Colliery explosion of 6 December 1875. *Barnsley Chronicle*, 18 March 1876, p. 8.

73 For more information on this case, see Holmes, *In Bed with the Victorians*, pp. 70–2.

74 Also sometimes referred to as Jane Mixon; *Chelmsford Chronicle*, 17 June 1870, p. 5; *Essex Herald*, 17 June 1870, p. 5.

4

Compromised spaces?

On a Sunday in October 1882, labourer John Bury returned home for breakfast following an early morning walk. After finishing his breakfast – a mutton chop and tea – Bury settled in a chair before the fire to smoke his pipe in the company of another man. However, the two men were soon interrupted by a 'scuffle' between a Mrs Whittaker and a Mrs McCormack. Getting 'half out of his chair', Bury pronounced, 'I'm not going to have this bother in my house.' To which Mrs McCormack retorted, 'Do you pay the rent of this house?' This was a rhetorical question. McCormack knew that Bury did not pay the rent, for he was not the tenant. That was Mrs Whittaker, the widow with whom Bury lodged and boarded. Bury's companion by the fireside was another of Whittaker's lodgers, labourer Michael Driscoll.[1]

Lodgers have long sat by the fireside. However, by the Victorian period, their presence became increasingly challenged as the middle class sought to define the home as a private family space. The idea of private family life was born in the early modern period. However, as Amanda Vickery outlines, only in the late eighteenth century did the desire for privacy become so firmly entrenched.[2] Before then, even the wealthiest householders had lived cheek-by-jowl with their extended kin, servants, and apprentices. However, industrialisation brought a burgeoning desire to separate home and work. For the middle classes, the ideal home was now a sanctuary from the hustle and bustle of the outside world.[3] Distinct lines began to be drawn between the public world and the private family, as summed up by the Registrar General, Major Graham, in the introduction of the 1851 census: 'The possession of an entire house is strongly desired by every Englishman: for it throws a sharp, well-defined circle round the family and hearth.'[4] The presence of lodgers such as Bury and Driscoll by the fireside compromised such firm lines drawn around the hearth and home. Indeed, to some, a lodger's presence in the home was 'evil'.[5]

Despite the widespread middle-class condemnation of the 'working-class' practice of taking lodgers, we know little about the lodger's place in these homes. Historians searching for the Victorian working-class lodger have caught sight of them in literature and autobiographies around the table or retreating to their own room. Thus, family and lodgers are either together or apart in these accounts. In this chapter, I explore whether working-class householders and their lodgers sought to create distinct lines between themselves through the organisation of the domestic dwelling lodging and their daily interactions, or whether, as the middle class feared, there were no lines drawn at all. Beginning with the exterior door, I examine the lodger's access to the threshold, revealing not only a boundary in the lodging arrangement but also to the outside world. Moving into the daily living spaces, I then explore how lodgers situated themselves in the household's everyday routines and rituals through their place at the table and fireside and the extent to which this positioning made them part of the family. Finally, climbing the staircase (as was usually, but not always the case) to bed, I outline a range of nocturnal accommodations in these usually cramped quarters, revealing that among the overcrowding, there nevertheless existed – with a few exceptions – sharp dividing lines when it came to the arrangement of sleeping bodies.

Crossing the threshold

The extent to which the middle class viewed the working-class home as the antithesis of the private family home started directly at the front door, where 'the open or absent door has become part of the conventional [narrative]'.[6] However, historians have shown that such a trope was far from typical. By the early nineteenth century, most householders had control over the thresholds of their homes. Among the working class, doors became commonly secured through the latch lock, preventing unwanted visitors.[7] Martin

Hewitt's re-reading of district visitors' accounts of visits to the slum found that 'Doors were sometimes locked against the visitor', and, in the cases 'where doors had no locks, it was not unusual … for door handles to be removed'.[8] Yet we know little about how this working-class practice of securing thresholds applied to the wanted guest: the lodger. The possession of a latchkey would have permitted lodgers to come and go as they pleased. Having built a relationship of trust with the householder over the months and years, long-term lodgers would almost certainly have been presented with a key. For example, George Henry Day had been lodging at No. 5 Exmouth Street, Southampton – the home of labourer Harry Berry and his wife, Ellen – for nearly two years, and having 'a latchkey' could 'let [himself] in'.[9] And, in 1888, before his death by suicide at his Islington lodgings of two years, John Fellows threw a parcel from his window containing 'the latchkey' to the house.[10]

Where lodgers were not privileged with a latchkey or such a mechanism was not in place, strict curfews might be imposed so that the house could be promptly shut up at nightfall, especially in urban areas where security was a more pressing concern. Twenty-three-year-old Richard Gould was an occasional lodger in the Islington home of shoemaker Charles and Mary Anne Allen. On one particular day, while staying at the Allens, Gould 'went out as usual [but] did not return until half-past seven o'clock in the evening'. Rebuked for his late arrival, Mrs Allen 'told him if he did not return home earlier [she] would not leave [her] door open for him'. Not finding such a request unreasonable, Gould responded: 'I expect that.'[11] More customary, lodgers would have to knock or shout on their late return.[12] This resulted in a late or disturbed night for at least one person. For example, widow Elizabeth Slack of No. 5 Labour-in-Vain Street, Shadwell, became a prominent witness in a coroner's inquest regarding an alleged murder because she had been 'about twenty minutes before one in the morning … sitting up waiting for her lodgers' when she heard a commotion outside the neighbouring house.[13] Other householders retired to bed, knowing that their sleep would be disturbed by a returning lodger. Lodgers' late nights were an imposition, if not a hazard, to those with whom they lodged. After locking up her home in Wakefield, Yorkshire, on a Saturday evening, seventy-five-year-old Sarah Ward proceeded to bed but would have to rise from her sleep to 'give admission to a lodger'. The lodger eventually arrived 'at a late hour' and, on proceeding to the door, Sarah fell down the stairs. Fracturing her skull, she never recovered from her injuries.[14]

Internally, however, dynamics over boundaries shifted when the lodger closed their room door. As John Styles demonstrates in his research on lodgings in eighteenth-century London, 'Some owners reported [in the Old Bailey proceedings] that after letting the room, they never entered it and hardly ever saw or heard the tenant. Many tenants had their own room key and kept their rooms locked.'[15] While the former – never seeing or hearing their tenants – was, as I establish below, untrue for the Victorian working-class domestic dwelling lodgings, evidence in the inquest reports nevertheless suggests an establishment of boundaries regarding the lodger's room, at least, that is, in the few cases where the lodger was privileged with their own room. Seventy-year-old statuary mason Samuel May – described by those who knew him as 'a very reserved man' – had lodged with the Haydons for four years, where his lodging room was his own space. The only reason Mrs Haydon had to venture into May's room was to clean it, but as noted in Chapter 3, he did his own cleaning, and as a result, she 'very seldom entered his room'.[16] Entrance, in several inquest reports, was noted to be gained only after knocking. For example, despite socialising with the woman with whom he lodged and another lodger, Thomas Morris alias Nash had a clearly established boundary to his own room. On the morning following his suicide, at 'About ten o'clock, his landlady, as was her practice, went to his room-door, and knocked at it. Not receiving any answer, she concluded he had gone out … entered the apartment.'[17]

Such privacy, however, was not just secured through customs but rather a key. For example, the parcel John Fellows threw from his window before his suicide not only contained a latchkey but also the key to his room, suggesting that the people with whom he lodged did not have a copy of the key. Sixty-four-year-old Royal Arsenal pensioner James Weller also appeared to be the only one in possession of a key to his lodging room, where, upon entering, he locked himself within. Even when Weller had caught fire in his room, only 'with great persuasion' on the part of the woman with whom he lodged did he unlock the door. Notably, the room where Weller slept was the ground floor parlour, which typically contained the householder's most prized possessions rather than a lodger and, therefore, was more likely to have a lockable door.[18] Such was the importance of a lockable door to some lodgers that – as David Churchill identifies in his work on crime and control in the city – some might apply 'creative solutions' such as 'a chair placed behind [the door] and taking the handle out the door and putting a nail over the latch'.[19] An inquest report I have come across outside the scope of this book's sample provides one such example. Sarah Amey, wife of James Amey, shoemaker, was called to give evidence at Sudbury's coroner's court pertaining to the suicide of sixty-five-year-old George Palmer – her lodger. Amey stated that Palmer 'had lived with herself and her husband' in their Suffolk home for 'about three months … On Friday morning, not hearing the deceased get up as usual, she sent her daughter to knock at his door, and, in getting no answer, her husband and a neighbour … broke open the door, which was fastened from the inside by a nail, the lock being broken.' According to the Amey, Palmer 'generally fastened his bedroom door at night'. Notably, in Palmer's case, his room could only be locked from the inside – possibly the case with a number of the inquests above also – and thus, when he was away from his room, a householder's access was possible.[20]

But why, where possible, did lodgers see fit to establish customary and physical boundaries to their rooms? To a certain extent, by securing the door from within, the lodger obtained a certain level of privacy, even personal freedom from the limits of living under someone else's roof. However, security seems to be the more practical reason for a lockable door. A lodger's unsecured room was an easy picking for dishonest householders searching for items to pawn. Ageing Huddersfield widow, Mrs Mary Crowther, took in several young male lodgers to maintain the roof over her head. However, their rent was not the only money Crowther lined her pockets with. Consumed by 'continual drinking', Mary – without her lodger's knowledge – 'pledged a pair of trousers and a shirt belonging to him, the proceeds of which [it was suggested] she had swallowed in beer and spirits'.[21] However, even the lockable room could be breached. In October 1851, the Backhouse family came to lodge with the bricklayer William Smith in his home in Guildford, Surrey, and were provided with – what they thought were – the only keys to their rooms. However, soon, they began to miss some of their possessions – 'rings, brooches, gold pins, lockets ... as well as small sums of money'. Suspecting Mrs Smith's daughter, Emma, a search was made of her bedroom, and under the floorboards, 'a great deal of things' were found, as well as 'three keys which fitted the locks [of the lodgers'] rooms'.[22]

Some lodgers also took opportunities to steal from other lodgers or, indeed, the householders. Exeter widow Jane Pinn was, it seems, plagued by light-fingered lodgers. One of Pinn's lodgers was fifty-eight-year-old laundress Jane Carnell. Recently separated from her husband, Carnell received 5s. a week from him in support, which quickly disappeared in drink. With her funds running dry, Carnell turned to pawning items. However, these items were not ones in her own possession. They belonged to lodger James Halse, who, on discovering some of his 'wearing apparel' was missing, confronted Carnell, who admitted to the theft.[23] Two months later, another of Pinn's lodgers – Emma Hill – stole a cash box, bed curtains, a blanket, four rings, three brooches, and other articles from Carnell's room.[24] Similarly, when wire worker Richard Heaton and his wife took Clara Kennedy as a lodger into their Warrington home, it was not long until items began to go missing. Looking all over, Mrs Heaton 'could not find her boots'. Mentioning this to Kennedy, she 'expressed some astonishment', but it was not long until the truth was uncovered. Kennedy had taken the boots and pawned them – under the name of Nellie Rice – for 2s. 6d. Promptly arrested, Kennedy died by suicide while in police custody.[25]

Around the table, by the fireside, in the public house

Lodgers who boarded, as many did, found their place at the family table, sharing both their food and utensils from breakfast through to supper. Indeed, the very act of getting one's feet under the table appeared to consolidate the lodger's place in the family circle. After maker-up of flax and yarn James Clarkson choked to death while eating breakfast, his wife, testifying before Preston's coroner, stated that 'all the family partook of it at breakfast' that day. The family also included their lodger.[26] Other breakfast scenes mimicked that of a husband and wife. In Shrawley, Worcestershire, Mary Ann Andrews, a widow aged seventy-one years, lived alone except for the presence of a lodger, labourer James Collins. Shortly before her death, 'The two breakfasted together in the kitchen at seven o'clock [before] Collins went to work.'[27] Such scenes were also replicated around the dinner and tea table.

Lodgers continued to blend into the domestic scene as evening drew in and the focal point of the working-class home shifted from the table to the fireside. Here, male inhabitants like Rory and Driscoll would spend their time at leisure – smoking a pipe, reading, or simply exchanging conversation. Male householders also kept company with their male lodger. In the hours preceding his death, sixty-seven-year-old Todmorden labourer William Wilkinson sat after tea reading his newspaper 'in the company with a lodger named Paul Judge'.[28] Of course, such cordiality between householders and lodgers was enforced in many ways through the fabric of the home. Most working-class homes, especially those that found it necessary to accommodate lodgers, would have had no additional living space to create some separation between householder and lodger. For example, Mrs Sarah Scorey took several lodgers into her Southampton home, but with 'not a separate sitting room ... the sitting room [was] used by Mrs Scorey and her lodgers'.[29]

But even where separation was possible, it was not always preferred. The evidence in the inquest reports suggests that of those lodgers who could retreat to their lodging room, many opted instead to spend their evenings in the company of the household and other lodgers. A jeweller by trade, Thomas Morris (alias Nash), cast out of the family home, found a de facto family in his lodgings. Accounting for the days leading up to his death, *London Daily Chronicle* reported, 'On Monday morning he went to see the execution of Sattler at Newgate' and then returned home to his lodgings where 'In the evening, he sat several hours with his landlady and a Mr Weston [another lodger] chatting and smoking his pipe' before he retired to 'his own room'. His companions noted, 'He was then quite cheerful.'[30] In another scene replicating that of husband and wife, on a cold January evening in Shrewsbury, Shropshire, seventy-four-year-old Elizabeth Howell '[sat] near the fire with her lodger, named Stanley' as he settled to smoke his pipe.[31]

Not all such domestic scenes with the lodger were so temperate. Jane Hamlett's work on CLHs of the same period highlights the hospitality or friendship of fellow lodgers through the sharing of drinks.[32] Unsurprisingly, then, alcohol was central to much of working-class householder–lodger conviviality, particularly involving – though not exclusively – male householders and male lodgers. The day before his death by suicide, Peckham chimney sweep Isaac James Wilkinson had been drinking in his brother's company and with his lodger 'named Crow'.[33] Similarly, Thomas Morris had also shared some beer, 'but not to excess', with the woman with whom he lodged and a fellow lodger in the hours before his suicide.[34] However, many of the inquest reports, rather unsurprisingly, record cases of drinking to excess, with various accounts of householders and lodgers partaking in – together – a 'spree' of drinking during Saturday nights, Sundays, and seasonal holidays.[35] For example, in Newcastle, when forty-nine-year-old Susannah Holden's clothes caught fire during a quarrel with miner Joseph Taylor (the man with whom she cohabited), the inquest following her death detailed the hours preceding the fatal incident. Taylor called before the coroner, stated himself, Holden, 'and a lodger named James Cavanagh … were in the house and drinking all day on Sunday [and] were more or less drunk in the afternoon and evening'. The lodger, refuting Taylor's statement, claimed he was 'perfectly sober' when he turned in for the night.[36] Yet sober or not, he did not deny he had spent his Sunday – the labouring man's day of leisure – socialising with the man and women with whom he lodged.

Alcohol also took the householder–lodger relationship outside of the domestic sphere, with householders and lodgers sometimes frequenting public houses together. Mrs Mary Ann Allen appears to have spent time with her lodgers in a public house near her home and, as one of her lodgers stated, 'we were all friends together'.[37] Such excursions were not always planned. On a Saturday evening in December 1882, fifty-two-year-old Marylebone shoemaker Joseph Hosking got word that his lodger – Mr Stone – had been arrested for being drunk and went to bail him out. Rather than scold him for the misdemeanour, the two men – accompanied by Hosking's wife Alice – 'went to a public house and got drinking together' before returning home 'slightly intoxicated'.[38] The Hoskings were not the only household to return home with their lodger in an intoxicated state. Following a fatal quarrel that led to the death of forty-nine-year-old labourer Arthur James Sallis, a witness at the inquest stated, 'On the [Friday] when [Sallis] received his injury, he and his wife and her mother and the lodger all came home "boozed," just after one o'clock' in the morning.[39] However, one of the most striking examples of how lodgers could be incorporated into the household's social life was their inclusion on family excursions, albeit one involving alcohol. Having hired a horse and trap, the Strout family headed out 'for a drive' along with bricklayer John Holdstock – their lodger. Having departed Faversham, the group partook in some refreshments when they arrived at Challock's Halfway House. The Strouts and Holdstock then proceeded to Ashford for dinner. By the time of their journey home – in a 'torrent of rain' – they were all somewhat the 'worse for liquor'.[40]

While alcohol consolidated the householder–lodger relationship in most cases, as was the case with all interpersonal relationships, alcohol could also fracture the relationship. While wagon builder William Petherham was a heavy drinker and frequently returned to his lodging drunk, the family with whom he lodged reported he 'was very quiet when drunk' and that he had, on at least one occasion, 'stopped out because he did not want to disturb' them.[41] Not all lodgers were so considerate. An excessively drunk lodger could be a significant and even dangerous burden on the household where they lodged. As well as cases of fatal fights taking place between male lodgers, householders could also have found themselves the target of drunken violence. Unmarried labourer John Last became a 'heavy drinker' over his fourteen years of lodging with the Vincents. In these latter years, Mrs Vincent was the target of his drunken rages. Indeed, as Vincent herself stated, Last's 'custom' was to ill-treat her when intoxicated and, such was the violence on some occasions, 'she had to fetch her husband'. But why, especially given Mrs Vincent's presence, did they allow Last to remain under their roof? As noted in Chapter 3, the Vincents could not have managed financially without their lodger.[42]

Noticeably, female lodgers are relatively absent from the evening scene of leisure, sitting – quite literally in some cases – quiet in the background. We only know of Sarah Ann Price's presence as a lodger in the home of Gloucester chimney sweep George Clements because she became caught in the crossfire of domestic violence. When Clements returned to his home on Union Street in a state of drunkenness and found 'no supper prepared', he began to quarrel with his wife. Taking up a large seashell, he threw it at her, missing and instead striking Price, who had been sitting on the sofa next to Clement's wife.[43] It is difficult to determine precisely why female lodgers were largely absent from the accounts of householder–lodger sociability, both inside and outside the home. To some extent, it is a matter of numbers. With far fewer female lodgers in the population overall, it simply means they would appear less frequently in the inquest reports. Or, perhaps, like working-class wives, their evenings were busied with domestic tasks that kept them from the scope of the coroner.

At night's close

We would expect the most significant compromise in living with lodgers came when retiring to bed for the night. Yet the inquest reports reveal most householders found a way to negotiate sleeping arrangements to provide some level of separation between themselves and their lodgers. In Victorian England, lodgers were generally absent in the overcrowded one-roomed dwelling. Indeed, according to the 1891 census, just 4 per cent of private homes accommodating lodgers comprised of one room.[44] Only in the most desperate circumstances did householders accommodate a lodger in such cramped quarters, for it was simply a matter of being unable to survive without them. Nottingham rat-catcher John Hope, whom we first met in Chapter 1, had little prospect of maintaining his family – a wife, unmarried daughter, and a married daughter and her three children – on his meagre and sporadic wages. And though their home was 'less than five yards square', two male lodgers lived and slept alongside them.[45] Similarly, when widow Francis Hatfield, as noted in Chapter 1, could no longer afford the rent on the room she shared with her dependent brother, her lodger 'allowed' her the 1s. a week rent for her single-room dwelling. For two members of the Hatfield home, at least, taking in a lodger also meant sharing a bed, for, as the inquest report regarding Hatfield's brother's death stated, there were just two beds. Unusually, the report does not extend to reporting who slept with whom.[46]

In the two-roomed dwelling, a lodger – when essential – could just about squeeze in with a realignment of space or bodies.[47] Sometimes, the family's living space would be transformed at night to accommodate a lodger. When Lily Bashman came to lodge in the Leeds home of tailor Mark Feinstein, 'she slept on a made-up bed in the lower room' while the family slept in the upper room (the only other room). This arrangement lasted for several months, only concluding when Feinstein murdered Bashman as she slept.[48] Meanwhile, as I have shown beyond the present book, a female lodger might be accommodated in the family's bedroom. Notably, while the coroner's court baulked at such a domestic arrangement, the family and lodger, in this case, appeared unperplexed by their situation. Indeed, for the lodger, sharing a bedroom with a family she knew was better than living with strangers.[49] Nonetheless, householders generally drew a line regarding accommodating male lodgers in this manner.

Where a male lodger was present in the two-roomed dwelling, sleeping arrangements would typically be rearranged according to sex. The male breadwinner, already having 'failed' in his role as a provider, could end up sharing a bed with the man they took in to make up his shortfall. With four children to maintain on a shoemaker's wages, finding a lodger in the Stafford home of Henry Murray Hall is hardly surprising. Perhaps a little more startling to our more modern associations of the bed with sex were the occupants of Hall's 'one bedstead'.[50] Instead of sharing the 'only' bedstead with the woman he called his wife, Mary Toft, Hall shared it with their lodger, fellow shoemaker John Cooper, while Mary and the children slept in the adjoining room.[51] A similar arrangement was also present in William Walton's two-roomed home. As noted in Chapter 1, being in a 'despondent state of mind', Walton did not work, and the family became increasingly dependent on their lodger – Fred Atkins – with whom Walton now shared the bedroom, while Ann and her daughters – the oldest being twelve – slept in the kitchen.[52]

We must not assume, however, that a lodger's presence in such cramped homes was a permanent arrangement. Instead, where familial sleeping arrangements were compromised, a lodger's presence tended to be temporary or occasional. In December 1888, the coroner for Shepton Mallet, Somerset, Mr W. Muller, encountered a home so 'wretched in the extreme, its squalor and overcrowded state being more characteristic of a populous city than a small town'. With their father out of work, the Drew family fell into destitution. Entirely dependent on the earnings of their older sons, who 'picked up a few shillings a week as labourers and errand boys', and their fourteen-year-old daughter's earnings as a factory hand, they took in an 'occasional' female lodger to help make ends meet. The inquest reports differ on the number of rooms in the Drews home, ranging between two and three, but what we do know is that the 'lower room was occupied at night by [the daughter], her father and mother, and a child of two or three years, and frequently a middle-aged lodger' who shared the daughter's bed – 'a roll of some sort'. The room or rooms upstairs were slept in 'by five or six boys', the Drews' sons.[53]

Beyond the two-roomed dwelling, lodgers could find a more permanent place in the home.[54] Nevertheless, the presence of a lodger still placed pressure on the family's own sleeping arrangements. For example, Mrs Cook's Worcester home, while described as a 'small' house, had three bedrooms, two of which were inhabited separately by lodgers – Mrs Butler and Mrs Burston. Mrs Cook and three children slept in the one remaining bedroom not given over to lodgers.[55] Likewise, Lancashire widow Betty Scott, having given over the front bedroom facing the street to lodgers, slept with her children and brother in the back bedroom. A third bedroom – the 'middle' room – acted quite literally as intermediate space, for this is where Betty sometimes shared a bed with her lodger-turned-paramour – a tragic tale to be returned to in Chapter 5.[56] Even extended families could find themselves crowded into one bedroom when the necessity for lodgers arose. The Stockport home of labourer John Loftus, known as a 'single' house, contained a cellar, houseplace (living space), and two bedrooms – one over the other. Despite its size, at least fifteen people lived under Loftus's roof: the first-floor bedroom had been given over to three male lodgers, while the top-storey bedroom 'but a few yards square ... contained no less than nine persons, all female, ranging from four months to 56 years'. We know from various inquest reports that the nine included Loftus's wife, Catherine; their daughters, Honor and Annie; and Loftus's daughter-in-law, Sarah, and her two young daughters. The other females in the room were not stated in the report.[57] However, the census taken just a year before a fatal fire ripped through Loftus's home suggests the other female inhabitants of the room were Loftus's unmarried daughter, Mary, his married daughter, Bridget Madden, and her young daughter. It might have also been the case that the family bedroom was not entirely off-limits to Loftus's lodgers, for the census also reveals twenty-one-year-old boarder Bridget Hardiman in their home. Certainly, it would have been more appropriate for her to sleep with the female family members than to bed down with the male lodgers.[58] One mystery, however, remains surrounding where the three male family members slept. Absent at the time of the fire, we can only speculate as to the room they called their bedroom.

The presence of a parlour or, indeed, parlours, alongside bedrooms, provided an opportunity for further revenue from lodgers. London chairmaker Edward George Pitt and his wife had taken in lodgers throughout their married life. After her death and as he aged, Pitt continued to take in lodgers, giving over several rooms of his house in Clarence Garden to lodgers while he and his daughter lived 'in the parlours'.[59] Whether the Pitts' own bedroom furniture had moved downstairs with them is not recorded. Certainly, Margaret Ponsonby's study of early-nineteenth-century inventories reveals the case of a middling-class widow, in reduced circumstances, who moved down to the parlour upon letting the upstairs to a lodger, taking her belongings with her – including a tent bedstead.[60] This was not, however, the case in the Cheshire home of chemical labourer James Deakin and his wife, Margaret. While few inquests detail how 'parlour-bedrooms' were furnished and arranged, a murder in the Deakin's home provides a glimpse into their nocturnal arrangements. Having taken in more lodgers than they had bedrooms and beds, the Deakins retreated to their parlour where they 'made up' a bed 'on a sofa and chairs'. Yet even in this room the Deakins were intruded on by a lodger, with Betsy Heald (also James's cousin, as noted in Chapter 3) sleeping on a mattress at the bottom of their makeshift bed.[61]

Parlours were, however, generally off-limits to sleeping lodgers. Lesley Hoskins's inventory study of home and work in the mid-nineteenth century uncovered, in one case, a press bedstead in the parlour of a lodging house belonging to engine fitter John Mabon. While Hoskins acknowledges 'There is no way of knowing how often or under what circumstances the press bedstead was used', she argues 'It was probably for family use since the light-finger was a common trope, and [Mabon's] parlour contained many easily removable items.'[62] Yet we find lodgers sleeping in parlours where this room served not as the 'best' room but as a surplus one. For

example, flour mill worker George Smith accommodated two
lodgers in his 'pretty six-roomed, white cemented house' in Ewell,
Surrey. One lodger, George Mason, slept in the upstairs back bedroom, while rail porter Ernest Smith slept in the front parlour.[63]
Widow Sarah McCleneghan arranged her Woolwich home along
similar lines, with dockyard pensioner James Harwood inhabiting
an upstairs bedroom and sexagenarian bachelor and Royal Arsenal
pensioner James Weller sleeping in the ground-floor parlour.[64]

Most lodgers, as noted above, slept in designated bedrooms.
Yet while a few lodgers were privileged with a room of their own,
in working-class homes – especially when it came to male lodgers – the lodger's bedroom was generally not for sole occupation.
The more lodgers that could be squeezed into a room, the more
income could be generated, necessary for those households lacking
the male breadwinner wage. At least two of widow Betty Scott's
male lodgers shared the front bedroom, while the three male lodgers in John Loftus's home also shared a room. Familiarity with their
nocturnal fellows certainly would have brought more ease to the
bedroom-sharing arrangement. Figure 4.1, No. 19 Portrack Street,
Stockton-on-Tees, was 'an ordinary working man's dwelling containing a sitting room and kitchen combined on the ground floor,
and two bedrooms above'.[65] However, no. 19 was not just occupied
by one ordinary working man, but four, John McManus, Thomas
Murphy, Nicholas Glancy, and James O'Neil – the lodgers of the
widow Mary Mahoney, all of whom shared the same bedroom. The
inquest report also reveals familiarity between some of these lodgers. Steel worker McManus might have only been lodging for 'the
past three weeks' in Mahoney's home, but as he reveals, he had
'known [his fellow lodger, O'Neil] for about 23 years'. Meanwhile,
Glancy and O'Neil were ironworkers noted to be 'on very friendly
terms', at least when drink was not involved.[66] Similarly, in the
two-up, two-down Burnley home of separated wife Mrs Mary Ann
Allen, her lodgers, Adam Robinson, Robert Chadwick and his two
young sons, and the man only known as 'Joe', all shared the upstairs
back bedroom. As noted in the previous chapter, both Robinson
and Chadwick were friends. 'Joe', however, was a stranger among
his fellow lodgers. They did not even know his surname.[67]

Some lodgers did not just share a bedroom. In struggling homes
where furnishings were in short supply, lodgers found themselves

Figure 4.1 The House, 19 Portrack Street. *Stockton Herald*, 20 October 1900, p. 5.

with a bed companion. Of course, as with bedroom sharing, such nocturnal intimacy might have been more comfortable when bedding down with those familiar to them. The 'very good friends' Charlotte Whale and Sarah Ellen Proctor, whom we have met in previous chapters, travelled, worked, lodged, and slept together.[68] Similarly, forty-five-year-old bachelor and wire bundler Richard Barrows and c. forty-six-year-old bachelor and general labourer John McDonald not only shared a bed in the Warrington home in which they lodged but, as noted in Chapter 3, also shared a family connection – they were both uncles of the man with whom they lodged.[69] Yet familiarity was not a prerequisite to sharing a bed in lodgings. When fifty-seven-year-old Leicester plumber William Horne arrived in Nottingham and took up lodgings in the home of accordion maker William Ward, he 'sle[pt] in the same bed' with garden labourer John Foster, Ward's other lodger. The two men appear to have been entirely strangers to each other.[70] This is not wholly unsurprising. In Victorian England's common lodgings houses, men slept cheek by jowl with perfect strangers, and, across the Channel, as Michelle Perrot observes, in the industrial towns such as Sedan in north-eastern France, single men with 'no familiar links to one another' lived in pensions at the cost of twenty-five or thirty francs a month, sleeping 'two to a bed'.[71]

Such close nocturnal proximity was not without its issues. Alongside the return of drunken lodgers, noise and the tussle for bedsheets could lead to a disturbed night's sleep for some lodgers. Forgeman Charles Henry Taylor and contractor's foreman James Carr 'slept in the same room' in Mark and Lily Smith's Dewsbury home. Yet neither man slept particularly well during the time they shared a room. As Carr informed the coroner's court after a fatal case of somnambulism, Taylor 'dreamed a good deal and talked in his sleep'.[72] And, in Workington, Cumberland, lodger Richard Thompson was perhaps one of the few bedsharing lodgers finding themselves cold at night. Sharing his bed with stone mason George Holmes, Thompson was continually disturbed in the night by the pulling of the covers and Holmes's mumblings. At the inquest held into Holmes's death, Thompson stated, 'I have lodged in the same house [as Holmes], and I have slept with him for the last four weeks. The last few nights he did not sleep well; he was very restless and pulled the clothes off the bed. Yesterday he slept badly. He sighed and breathed very heavy ... talking rather curiously' as he slept.[73]

However, a room to themselves would not have necessarily brought the lodger a better night's sleep. Deborah Willis and John Last hired a room of their own in their respective lodgings, though neither were what we would call habitable. When the surgeon attending to John Last entered his lodging room – the top floor room in the Ipswich home of Mr and Mrs Vincent – he found a room 'more like a closet than a bedroom, bare – absolutely bare, save for one box, the dead man's – without a fire-place, cheerless, and ... frightfully cold – as cold as in open air'.[74] His iron bedstead 'was only half-covered with the mattress, and [his] legs were on the bare irons; there were some dirty things over him' acting as bedclothes.[75] Deborah Willis, whom we first meet in Chapter 2, may have solely occupied an unfurnished lodging room in nearby Colchester, but it was similarly sparse and plagued by an infestation. 'The bedstead, which was covered with vermin, had been taken down to be cleaned ... at [Willis's] request ... After it was taken down, [Willis and her youngest child] slept on a few shavings in a bag on the floor.' Her only bedclothes comprised of 'two old sheets and a quilt' and 'two pillows' supplied by the woman with whom she lodged.[76]

Conclusion

Having gained access through the front door, the lodger wove into the domestic scene of many Victorian working-class homes, from their rare presence in overcrowded one-room dwellings or occasional presence in the cramped two-roomed dwelling where realignment of the home was necessary to their commonplace presence in the three- and four-roomed ordinary working man's house. Incorporated into daily life, many ate around the family table, sat by the fireside, smoking a pipe, discussing the day's news, or sharing a drink – mimicking, in many cases, a familial domestic scene. Yet as night closed in, sharp delineations were made between family and lodgers when it came to sleeping arrangements. While in the poorest homes, male and female lodgers might be found sleeping cheek-by-jowl with at least one family member, lodgers and householders generally did not share a bedroom. This is not to say most lodgers, as a consequence, got a bedroom to themselves. Rather, most lodgers shared a bedroom with other lodgers and, in some cases, a bed.

Sharing a home with lodgers was not without its issues. Security was sometimes breached and, alongside drink cementing cordial relations, drunk and violent lodgers could pose a threat to fellow lodgers and householders alike, while lodgers returning home late or being noisy could bring a disturbed night's sleep. Meanwhile, where clear lines were drawn in the sleeping arrangements between lodger and householder to prevent their intrusion on the bedroom, many of these families, as a consequence, found themselves – as opposed to the lodgers they accommodated – sleeping in overcrowded bedrooms and, on occasion, displaced from sleeping quarters entirely.

However, despite their incorporation into household and family life, the lodger – as the opening example demonstrates – had little authority over the space they called home. For male lodgers, in particular, this sat at odds with the Victorian expectations of their gender. While the male lodger's place at the table, at the fireside, and at the public house mimicked that of the breadwinner, they remained emasculated. The result of this, as I demonstrate in the next chapter, led some male lodgers to seek the place of the dominant male in their lodgings by looking for a place in the female householder's bed.

Notes

1 *Preston Herald*, 28 October 1882, p. 6; *Blackburn Standard*, 21 October 1882, p. 3. In some newspaper articles, he is listed as John Rory. However, he is generally referred to as John Bury in the newspapers and other historical records. TNA, RG11/4200, f. 39, p. 13, s. 325, 1881 England, Wales & Scotland Census.

2 Amanda Vickery, 'An Englishman's Home Is His Castle? Thresholds, Boundaries and Privacies in the Eighteenth-Century London House', *Past & Present*, 199:1 (2008), 148–9. DOI: 10.1093/pastj/gtn006. Also see Beatrice Moring, 'Introduction: Lodgers in Rural and Urban Europe in the Past', *Continuity and Change*, 31:1 (2016), 1. DOI: 10.1017/S0268416016000072.

3 Leonore Davidoff, Megan Doolittle, Janet Fink, and Katherine Holden, *The Family Story: Blood, Contract, and Intimacy, 1830–1960* (London: Longman, 1999), pp. 178–80; Vickery, 'An Englishman's Home', 148.

4 Cited in Leonore Davidoff, 'The Separation of Home and Work? Landladies and Lodgers in Nineteenth- and Twentieth-Century England', in Sandra Burman (ed.), *Fit Work for Women* (London: Croom Helm, 1979), pp. 68–74.

5 Leonore Davidoff explains that taking in a lodger was 'a sign that the family could no longer be kept private and implied a loss of caste'. Davidoff, 'The Separation of Home and Work', p. 71.

6 Martin Hewitt, 'District Visiting and the Constitution of Domestic Space in the Mid-Nineteenth Century', in Janet Floyd and Inga Bryden (eds), *Domestic Space: Reading the Nineteenth-Century Interior* (Manchester: Manchester University Press, 1999), pp. 130–1.

7 Hewitt, 'District Visiting', p. 129; Vickery, 'An Englishman's Home', 171.

8 Hewitt, 'District Visiting', pp. 130–1.

9 *Hampshire Advertiser*, 3 January 1900, p. 3.

10 *Islington Gazette*, 1 October 1888, p. 3. Odell's latch key was invented c.1792. An image can be viewed here: https://collection.sciencemuseumgroup.org.uk/objects/co50516/odells-latch-key-invented-c-1792–key (accessed 19 August 2024).

11 *Morning Chronicle*, 19 March 1840, p. 3.

12 Something Amanda Vickery also observed in eighteenth-century lodgings – Vickery, 'An Englishman's Home', 161.

13 *Morning Post*, 11 June 1846, p. 7.

14 *Leeds Times*, 30 May 1846, p. 8.

15 John Styles, 'Lodging at the Old Bailey: Lodgings and their Furnishing in Eighteenth-Century London', in John Styles and Amanda Vickery (eds), *Gender, Taste and Material Culture in Britain and North America, 1700–1830* (New Haven, CT: Yale University Press, 2006), p. 70.

16 *Islington Gazette*, 2 February 1888, p. 3.

17 *London Daily Chronicle*, 20 February 1858, p. 3.

18 *Kentish Independent*, 2 September 1876, p. 8; *Kent & Sussex Courier*, 1 September 1876, p. 6; Lesley Hoskins, 'Stories of Work and Home in the Mid-Nineteenth Century', *Home Cultures*, 8:2 (2011), 151–69. DOI: 10.2752/175174211X12961586699720.

19 David Churchill, *Crime Control and Everyday Life in the Victorian City: the Police and the Public* (Oxford: Oxford University Press, 2018), p. 130.

20 *Ipswich Journal*, 19 September 1871, p. 3.

21 *Huddersfield Chronicle*, 27 February 1864, p. 8.

22 *Sussex Advertiser*, 24 February 1852, p. 7.

23 *Exeter & Plymouth Gazette*, 18 July 1876, p. 2.

24 *Exeter & Plymouth Gazette*, 5 September 1876, p. 3; *Exeter & Plymouth Gazette*, 9 September 1876, p. 4; *Exeter & Plymouth Gazette*, 20 October 1876, p. 3.

25 *Liverpool Mercury*, 10 August 1888, p. 6; TNA, RG11/3795, f. 111, p. 27, s. 874, 1881 England, Wales & Scotland Census.

26 *Ulverston Mirror & Furness Reflector*, 12 March 1864, p. 7; *Preston Herald*, 12 March 1864, p. 10.

27 *Worcester Journal*, 20 October 1894, p. 3.

28 *Todmorden & District News*, 5 January 1900, p. 5.

29 *Hampshire Advertiser*, 17 January 1846, p. 3.

30 *London Daily Chronicle*, 20 February 1858, p. 3.

31 *Shrewsbury Chronicle*, 16 January 1852, p. 4.

32 Jane Hamlett, *At Home in the Institution: Material Life in Asylums, Lodging Houses and Schools in Victorian and Edwardian England* (Basingstoke: Palgrave Macmillan, 2015), pp. 111–12.

33 *Lambeth and Southwark Advertiser*, 8 May 1858, p. 2.
34 *London Daily Chronicle*, 20 February 1858, p. 3.
35 Brian Harrison, *Drink and the Victorians: The Temperance Question in England, 1815–1872* (Staffordshire: Keele University Press, 1994), pp. 290–308.
36 *Newcastle Journal*, 31 March 1882, p. 3.
37 *Burnley Express*, 14 July 1894, p. 8.
38 *Marylebone Mercury*, 9 December 1882, p. 2.
39 *Gloucestershire Echo*, 12 October 1900, p. 4.
40 *Kentish Independent*, 26 November 1864, p. 8; *Kentish Chronicle*, 3 December 1864, p. 4.
41 *Derbyshire Courier*, 15 July 1900, p 6.
42 *Ipswich Journal*, 6 January 1894, p. 2.
43 Price eventually succumbed to her injuries, and Clements was charged with manslaughter: Gloucester *Journal*, 26 November 1870, p 6. Notably, the incident did not deter other women from lodging in the Clements' home, with two female lodgers present when Clements was out on bail. TNA, RG10/2617, f. 25, p. 44, s. 238, 1871 England, Wales & Scotland Census. After serving just six calendar months, with hard labour, for manslaughter, Clements returned home. *Gloucester Journal*, 8 April 1871, p. 3. But this was to be the first of several spells in prison. In late 1875, Clement served another sentence for assaulting his wife. However, this time, he returned to an empty home. Once again, Clements resorted to taking in young females as lodgers, subletting his home to Lilly Cook and Sarah Bryant at 5s. a week each. However, the situation soon soured. Becoming infatuated with Cook but finding his advances rebuffed, Clements became increasingly jealous. Returning from the public house one evening, he stabbed Cook. Cook survived, but Clements was sentenced to twenty years of penal servitude this time. *Gloucestershire Chronicle*, 11 December 1875, p. 5; *Gloucestershire Chronicle*, 18 December 1875, p. 2; *Gloucester Journal*, 30 December 1876, p. 7.
44 Kevin Schürer and Edward Higgs, Integrated Census Microdata (I-CeM), 1851–1911. [data collection]. UK Data Service. SN: 7481 (2020). DOI: 10.5255/UKDA-SN-7481-2.
45 *Nottingham Journal*, 6 April 1864, p. 3. To provide some context, Hope's home would have been little more than the size of today's average garden shed.
46 *London Daily Chronicle*, April 2, 1870, p. 6.
47 In the 1891 census, the presence of lodgers in two-room dwellings was also relevantly low, just 14 per cent. Schürer & Higgs, I-CeM, 1851–1911.

48 *Leeds Mercury*, 6 November 1900, p. 6; *Shields Daily News*, 6 November 1900, p. 3.

49 For more information on this case, see Vicky Holmes, 'Accommodating the Lodger: The Domestic Arrangements of Lodgers in Working-Class Dwellings in a Victorian Provincial Town', *Journal of Victorian Culture*, 19:3 (2014), 322–4. DOI: 10.1080/13555502.2014.947181.

50 Vicky Holmes, 'Pulling Back the Covers: Uncovering Beds in the Victorian Working-Class Home', in Joseph Harley, Vicky Holmes, and Laika Nevalainen (eds), *The Working Class at Home, 1790–1940* (Cham: Palgrave Macmillan, 2022), pp. 73–95.

51 *Staffordshire Advertiser*, 3 July 1858, p. 3.

52 *Bradford Daily Telegraph*, 8 March 1870, p. 4; *Shields Gazette & Daily Telegraph*, 8 March 1870, p. 4.

53 *Weston Mercury*, 22 December 1888, p. 8; *Western Gazette*, 21 December 1888, p. 3.

54 Aside from the various issues with the accuracy regarding the number of rooms recorded on the 1891 household schedules, they too demonstrate the prevalence of lodgers in the three- and four-roomed dwellings – 24 per cent in three-room dwellings, 57 per cent in four-room dwellings. Schürer and Higgs, I-CeM, 1851–1911. For more information on the GRO's attempts to enumerate the number of rooms on household schedules, see Edward Higgs, *Making Sense of the Census Revisited* (London: HMSO, 2005), pp. 69–70.

55 *Cheltenham Journal*, 12 November 1864, p. 8. Given the size of the house, it would be fair to speculate that, at some point, a partition wall might have been added to one of the bedrooms to create the third bedroom. Her husband, Robert, an attorney's clerk, appears to have left his wife, leaving her to fall into difficult circumstances necessitating a lodger, for he is neither present on the night of the inquest nor in the following census, where he is living as a lodger elsewhere in the town. TNA, RG10/3049, f. 37, p. 14, s. 92, 1871 England, Wales & Scotland Census.

56 *Burnley Express*, 7 January 1882, p. 6.

57 *Manchester Courier*, 17 April 1882, pp. 5, 8; *Nottinghamshire Evening News*, 17 April 1882, p. 3; Manchester Evening News, 18 April 1882, p. 2; Cheshire Observer, 22 April 1882, p. 7; Manchester Times, 22 April 1882, p. 3.

58 TNA, RG11/3477, f. 79, p. 26, s. 701, 1881 England, Wales & Scotland Census.

59 *Daily News* (London), 25 March 1876, p. 3 TNA, HO107/1493, f. 593, p. 25, s. 130, 1851 England, Wales & Scotland Census; TNA, RG09/97, f. 12, p. 19, s. 128, 1861 England, Wales & Scotland Census; TNA, RG10/204, f.14, p. 20, s. 131, 1871 England, Wales & Scotland Census.

60 Margaret Ponsonby, *Stories from Home: English Domestic Interiors 1750–1850* (Aldershot: Ashgate, 2007), pp. 132–3.

61 *Cheshire Courant*, 31 January 1894, p. 5; *Cheshire Observer*, 3 February 1894, p. 6; *Chester Courant*, 14 February 1894, p. 5.

62 Hoskins, 'Stories of Work and Home', 160–1.

63 *Surrey Comet*, 25 December 1869, p. 1; *Lloyd's Weekly Newspaper*, 26 December 1869, p. 12; *Surrey Advertiser*, 1 January 1870, p. 3.

64 *Kentish Independent*, 2 September 1876, p. 8; *Kent & Sussex Courier*, 1 September 1876, p. 6. McCleneghan's husband had also been a Royal Arsenal pensioner. TNA RG10/784, f. 37, p. 13, s. 94, 1871 England, Wales & Scotland Census.

65 In the 1891 census, Mary Mahoney lists her occupation as a lodging housekeeper. Yet as the inquest reports reveal, no. 19 Portrack Street bore little resemblance to a lodging house as we would expect it to be. TNA, RG12/4052, f. 61, p. 10, s. 46, 1891 England, Wales & Scotland Census.

66 *Stockton Herald*, 20 October 1900, p. 5.

67 *Burnley Express*, 16 June 1894, p. 8.

68 *Middlesex Independent*, 21 April 1888, p. 3.

69 *Runcorn Advertiser*, 23 February 1900, p. 6; TNA, RG13/3581, f. 7, p. 6, s. 26, 1901 England, Wales & Scotland Census.

70 *Nottinghamshire Guardian*, 21 January 1876, p. 8.

71 Michelle Perrot, *The Bedroom*, trans. L. Elkin (New York: Yale University Press, 2018), p. 185.

72 *Batley News*, 15 September 1900, p. 2. Some newspaper reports refer to Taylor's occupation as 'bargeman'.

73 *Whitehaven News*, 1 September 1864, p. 6.

74 *East Anglian Daily Times*, 4 January 1894, p. 5; *Ipswich Journal*, 6 January 1894, p. 2.

75 *Ipswich Journal*, 6 January 1894, p. 2.

76 *Essex Standard*, 15 April 1864, p. 6.

5

Beyond the boundaries

Busy with washing, Betty Scott was startled by a sharp, quick, bold, confident rap. Hastily drying her hands, the young widow approached the door to be greeted on the front step by a tall, powerfully and proportionally built man with a heavy moustache and whiskers. 'I'm Robert Templeton. I've come 'bout the lodgings', the bachelor declared. 'Come in', beckoned Betty. As he stooped to enter her home, Betty immediately sensed a change in fortune. Had this been the opening scene of a Victorian music-hall entertainment or a Dickens or Swepstone novel, what would have followed would have been Betty's 'embarrassing romantic pursuit of a resistant lodger'.[1] As Nadine Muller discusses, such works frequently portrayed romantic liaisons between lone male lodgers and their widowed landladies as a relationship pursued by the bereaved woman to fill 'the vacant space left by the departed spouse'.[2] The lodger, a victim, is entrapped and devoured by his desperate – if not delusional – landlady.[3] However, Betty's story is not one of fiction but a tale of reality revealed in the Victorian coroner's court and one that took a very different trajectory from that portrayed in popular culture. Although I have taken artistic license with the story of how Templeton arrived in Betty's home as a lodger, we know from the inquest reports that – alongside his physical description – within weeks, Templeton's position shifted from one of a lodger to a lover.[4] Yet the evidence of the coroner's court reveals that the courtship had not been a result of the widow's relentless wearing down of an unwitting lodger. Instead, it was the male lodger in a tireless pursuit of the young widow with whom he lodged – a pursuit with a tragic ending, as we will see shortly.

Fuelled by Victorian music hall and literature and, by the twentieth century, postcards, historians have long speculated on the opportunities for sexual relationships between the female householder and her lodger.[5] Yet finding evidence of these relationships beyond the literary and anecdote has received little scholarly attention. Most irregular relationships that took place behind closed doors remain out of view, except, that is, when they become a matter of legal proceedings. As Ginger S. Frost's work has shown, criminal proceedings pertaining to violence provide abundant details on irregular unions among the working class, including those formed between wives and lodgers. Lodgers, after all, were not just taken in by widows. Frost's research on adulterous cohabitations – a large consequence of the prohibitive costs of divorce proceedings – reveals how some working-class wives, compelled to take in lodgers after their husbands were committed to asylums or prisons, did go on to cohabit with a lodger to ease the financial and emotional burden of life without a male breadwinner.[6] Moreover, as I have shown elsewhere, the records of the Victorian coroner's court throw open the door to the most intimate details of working-class 'marriage' in its various guises. Indeed, this is where I first begin to question our current narratives surrounding the sexual relationships formed between widows and their male lodgers.[7]

Building on Frost's and my previous discoveries in the coroners' inquests, in this chapter, I explore a range of widow–lodger and wife–lodger relationships that crossed expected boundaries to understand further how these relationships played out in reality. First, turning to female-headed households – namely, those run by widows and estranged wives – I examine the circumstances in which these relationships formed with lodgers and the strained power dynamics that shaped them. Secondly, heading into the male-headed home – where the male lodger was generally a welcome (if somewhat also inconvenient) presence – I explore the potentially destabilising presence of the male lodger in the marital home and its violent consequences. Whether widow or wife, however, I reveal that relationships between women and their lodgers, at least those coming before Victorian coroners, were more tragedy than comedy.

Widows, estranged wives, and lodgers

There is no denying that some widows saw potential husbands in the men who came to lodge under their roof. For working-class women, bereavement was an emotional *and* material tragedy.[8] The loss of the male breadwinner placed grieving households on the brink of destitution. To survive, alongside the galling experience of applying for parochial relief that provided all but the bare minimum, young widows had to find further means to support their families.[9] As I discussed in Chapter 1, laundry and lodgers were a prominent source of income among such women. Yet with their days filled with toil, it left little time for, as Muller coins, 'husband hunting'. Therefore, for some, the male lodger represented an opportunity to return to the status quo.[10] Mary Sloper née Webb, left with four young children to support, married one of her lodgers – Henry Burdock – while still in the shadow of grief, for just over a year had elapsed between her husband's death and her second marriage. We cannot know the reasonings behind Mary's prompt decision to remarry, although economic factors undoubtedly pulled her in that direction. Yet Mary Sloper's transition to Mary Burdock proved a cautionary tale to other widows contemplating marriage with a male lodger.

Working-class women were all too well aware that a bad choice of husband placed a significant burden upon their shoulders. In her haste to marry her lodger, Mary Sloper soon learned – as we saw in Chapter 1 – that a rise in status from lodger to husband did not always entail an elevation from paying guest to provider. It is no surprise then to find caution among widows contemplating marriage with their lodgers-turned-lovers. Widow Betty Scott was, if anything, cautious about her relationship with her lodger, calico printer Robert Templeton. Considered a 'most industrious, clean, and laborious' woman in the community and, having remained a faithful widow for over a decade, Betty continued to receive parish support long after her husband's death.[11] Yet such relief would cease if the Poor Law Guardians caught wind of a potential husband.[12] Therefore, Betty endeavoured to conceal the courtship. Indeed, so closely guarded was the relationship that another of her lodgers, Edward Carling, had been living under her roof for some weeks before he realised Scott and Templeton were on 'intimate terms'.

Nonetheless, the presence of a man in her home, who, as one news-paper report stated, 'always gained the admiration of those who saw him on account of his splendid physique', meant that rumours soon abounded in the village of a forthcoming wedding. How could then Betty deny him? Yet she did. Templeton was, witnesses stated, intent on marriage, but Betty repeatedly refused him. In this refusal, as Frost examines in relation to working-class cohabitation, Betty left the door open to change her mind. And that is exactly what she did when she discovered Templeton was far from a suitable replace-ment for her deceased husband.[13] Betty ended the relationship when Templeton lost his employment due to his intemperate habits. Then, reasserting her position as the head of the household, she gave him 'notice to leave her lodgings'. However, as Frost also outlines, the lack of a marriage contract did not mean relationships could be ended without incident.[14] In this instance Betty, tied to her former paramour through the lodging contract, a matter returned to in the next chapter, could not immediately turn Templeton out of her home. Tragically, the notice period allowed him to exert revenge. Spurred on by suspicions that Betty was forming an intimacy with another lodger – to which there appears no foundation, but as Frost demonstrates, unfounded jealously was commonplace in irregular unions – he crept into the back bedroom Betty shared with her chil-dren and brother and cut her throat as she slept.[15]

Typically, irregular unions among the working class left women with little power and security.[16] Yet female householder–male lodger relationships that tipped into the sexual saw the power dynam-ics reversed. When lodgers formed sexual relationships with the women with whom they lodged, as seen with Betty, they still lived under *her* roof. Without the legal bonds of matrimony, the male remained subordinate in her home, never entirely shedding their status as a lodger and instead sitting somewhere between lover and lodger. Indeed, in some homes, such men became known as the 'boss lodger', as revealed in a coroner's inquest held twelve years later just a stone's throw from Betty's home. William Crossley was no stran-ger to forming sexual relations with the women he lodged with. In his early forties, Crossley – having lived in lodgings in Burnley throughout his adult life – came to lodge with forty-six-year-old widow Sarah Bowes on Lydia Street, and soon after that, they wed. The marriage, however, was short-lived. Sarah died just two years later. Packing up his furniture and other belongings, Crossley – as discussed in Chapter 2 – found lodgings with former neighbour Mrs Mary Ann Allen. Once again, Crossley's relationship with the woman he lodged soon crossed the boundaries of the householder–lodger relationship. His fellow lodgers observed that 'He regularly gave his wages to Mrs Allen, went shopping with her, and treated her in every way as a man should treat his wife', including sharing her bed. Yet she was not his wife, nor could she be, for Allen – while separated from her husband – was still legally married and, like others in her position, did not have the financial means to dissolve the union even if she wished.[17] Therefore, Crossley assumed the position of 'boss lodger', as he was known among his fellow lodgers.

Such an impasse in the relationship, however, led to tensions. Quarrels frequently disturbed neighbours, and on one particular occasion that saw Crossley turned out by Allen, Crossley broke a window. Symbolic, perhaps, of the blurred boundaries in their relationship. It was not long, however, until Crossley was returned to the position as the boss lodger, and the couple 'resumed the quarrelsome life'. The tipping point came when Allen's daughter returned to live with her mother. Objecting to Crossley's presence, she pleaded with her mother to end the relationship and send Crossley packing. All this fuelled Crossley's paranoid state. He became convinced that Allen's daughter and his fellow lodgers were 'conspirators whose object was to remove him from his position as "boss lodger"' and replace him with another. Fearing she would lose her other lodgers as a result of Crossley's increasingly volatile behaviour, she gave him notice to quit her home. After all, even despite his elevated status as 'boss lodger', Crossley was still a lodger and had to live by such terms. On the day Crossley was served his final meal in her home, he had gone into the cellar, retrieved an axe, hid it under his jacket, and returned to the kitchen to join his fellow lodgers. Moments later, Crossley began his murderous attack, an ordeal that Allen did not survive. The coroner's jury, heavily steered by the coroner, returned a verdict of wilful murder.[18] Notably, at the following assize trial, Crossley's defence – pushing for a manslaughter verdict – argued that he had been provoked by Allen and her daughter's 'constant nagging' and warranted jealousy and, crucially, had committed the act while intoxicated. However, like Templeton before him, Crossley was found guilty of murder and sentenced to death.[19]

While female householders may have held the cards in the relationship financially and domestically, when the relationship tipped into violence, they lost all their power.

Not every female householder–lodger relationship that shifted from platonic to sexual was consensual. Contrary to popular depictions, some of the inquest reports point to relationships of a coercive nature between female householders and their male lodgers, but these were not tales of women preying on their lodgers but rather of lodgers preying on the women with whom they lodged. Behind closed doors, lone females could find themselves vulnerable to the unwanted advances from the men they depended on for survival. Louisa Ferris, whom we first meet in Chapter 1, was forced to take in lodgers after the end of her volatile marriage. Just twenty-six years old, she soon found herself the object of a lodger's attention. Policeman Patrick White appeared determined to cross the boundaries of the householder–lodger relationship, whether Louisa consented or not. At the inquest into White's death, it was recorded that White 'had before made overtures of an improper nature to her, which she more than once rejected, and there is too much reason to believe that he finally accomplished her ruin by means of drugged liquors. After a time, she became pregnant by him [and] he prevailed upon her to adopt the means for procuring abortion.' On the night of White's death, another lodger, Elizabeth Jones, who slept alone in the backroom, woke to find White standing over her bed. Suggestions were made that – after an evening of drinking – White had also determined to engage in suspected non-consensual sexual contact with Jones but had been disturbed by Louisa. The following morning, he was dead at Louisa's hands. Despite the evidence of coercion presented at the inquest, at the following criminal trial, the judge recoiled at the jury's verdict of manslaughter and sought fit to rebuke Louisa. Seeing only her relationship with White as one of adultery, he believed that one sin led her onto the path of another – adultery was a mere stepping stone to murder. The judge sentenced Louisa to be transported to Van Diemens Land 'for the term of her natural life'.[20] As will be seen below, this far exceeds the sentences handed out to the men who had killed their lodgers.

In many cases, knowing the exact nature of the relationships behind closed doors is difficult, especially when there are no direct witnesses. Rhoda Bond also appears to have suffered the unwanted attention of her male lodgers. Soon after the death of her husband, Bond took in Frank Lloyd – a bit-maker and filer – as a lodger in her Walsall home. Confusion soon abounded as to the true nature of the relationship, with some believing Lloyd to have established his place as lodger-paramour. With no one else living under Bond's roof, there was no one to attest to the true nature of the relationship and what exactly went on behind Bond's closed door. One neighbour's testimony suggests, however, that the relationship was one-sided:

> Eliza Walker, 410, Park Brook, said she and her husband went into Mrs Bond's about nine o'clock on Saturday night [shortly before the fateful event]. Bond and Lloyd seemed on good terms, and he made the pretence of kissing her. Witness said, 'I don't want to see anything of that falseness: if you are the same behind folk's back as in their presence it is different.' Lloyd asked her husband for some tobacco and he gave it. Lloyd was quite 'fresh'. Mrs. Bond was quieter than usual … and it seemed as if there was something the matter. She kept pointing to her bosom, and witness thought she was motioning about a blow he had given her some time before. When she and her husband left, Mrs. Bond bolted the door after them.

Reading between the lines of Eliza Walker's testimony, Bond appears to have been victim to the unwanted attentions of her lodger and fearful of the harm he might yet inflict upon her body, covertly signalling to her neighbour a cry for help that went unheeded.[21] Just a few hours later, Bond was dead. She told several witnesses as she lay dying that Lloyd had 'pushed or hit her' as she ascended the stairs, causing her to fall and the lamp that she was carrying to break and ignite her dress. Having made it out of the house and into the yard, witnesses stated that Lloyd merely watched on as neighbours attempted to extinguish the flames. On hearing the evidence, the coroner's jury determined a verdict of manslaughter, and Lloyd was committed for trial, where he was found 'not guilty'. While there was evidence of his prior violent actions, there was sufficient 'reasonable doubt' as to exactly what occurred on that fateful night.[22]

Wives and lodgers

Taking a lodger into the marital home could be a double-edged sword. While it alleviated the family's immediate financial distress, the lodger signalled the husband/father's failure to provide. Indeed, as Davidoff argues, the male head was metaphorically gelded by the presence of a male lodger, throwing the home into disorder.[23] Victorian music hall, in particular, played on the idea of the lodger as a threat to the marital home, such as the song 'Our Lodger's Such a Nice Young Man' (1897). In reality, it is safe to say that most wives did not throw themselves into their male lodger's arms. As is well acknowledged, working-class women tended to remain even in the most unhappy and volatile of marriages.[24] And, of course, at this time, to commit adultery as a woman was to tarnish one's reputation for life. Even if temptation came their way, married women accommodating lodgers – as Robert Roberts notes in his account of growing up in a classic slum – were well aware of the scrutiny they came under from neighbours: 'Did the husband ever leave his missus with the lodger. If so, at what time and how long?'[25] Nevertheless, even without the intrusion of adultery, the male lodger could be a destabilising presence in homes where tensions were already heightened.

Taking a male lodger in itself fuelled resentment among some husbands. In close quarters, a feeling of emasculation could tip into grievous jealousy. Charlotte Ball – whom we met in Chapter 1 – in consequence of her husband's 'intemperate and idle habits', had taken in a male lodger, Alfred Smith. Cramped conditions meant, however, that he slept in the family bed – an unusual domestic arrangement that soon brought further strife to an already unhappy home. Charlotte's husband protested at his wife and Smith remaining in bed when he got up for breakfast and even began complaining to neighbours about his 'wife's conduct'. Increasingly convinced his wife 'showed a marked preference for the lodger', Ball determined to punish her for the supposed misdemeanour by drowning their son in the Thames Valley canal. Later, when challenged with the fact that neighbours spoke well of his wife, John Ball did not respond. No evidence was ever brought forward of adultery.[26] Such a tragedy resulting from unfounded jealousy burgeoning in close quarters was far from isolated. As noted in Chapter 4, William Walton – out of work due to 'a despondent mind' – shared the family's only bed with their lodger, Fred Atkins, while his wife, Ann, and their daughter slept in the kitchen. Such proximity, however, only served to aggravate Walton's state of mind. Almost immediately, 'Walton suspected that an improper intimacy existed between his wife and lodger', a suspicion that appeared to have little foundation. Nevertheless, 'Determined on a most horrible revenge' for the wrong he believed had been done to him, Walton took a razor from the drawers and 'made a savage [and fatal] attack upon his wife'. Walton then burst into the bedroom where Atkins was sleeping following a night shift, and a scuffle ensued between the men. Escaping, Atkins was able to raise the alarm, but not before the Walton daughter returned home to find her mother and father both lying dead. The coroner's jury concluded that William had killed his wife and then died by suicide.[27]

Of course, some suspicions were warranted. As one judge stated, according to Robert Roberts, in the early twentieth century, lodgers, selfishness, and greed were the most common causes of marital breakup.[28] Indeed, some inquest reports confirm adultery between married women and their male lodgers, along with the thousands of elopement cases reported in the Victorian press.[29] Of those cases of adultery between lodgers and married women heard before the Victorian coroner's court – an inquest being occasioned by the death of at least one of the party – the lodger appeared to have presented an escape route from a regretted union. Just months into their marriage, agricultural labourer Jasper Wells found himself alone after his wife, Miriam Kate – better known as Jessie – eloped with their lodger, agricultural labourer Albert Sands.[30] When Hannah Gough wed James Taylor, she was 'little more than 15 whilst he was 35'; a twist in this story is that her husband – as one newspaper reported – had previously cohabited with her mother, and Hannah soon came to rue the marriage.[31] She told her mother 'she did not like him, and never should', hardly surprising when, at such a young age, she found herself cooking and cleaning for upwards of ten lodgers at a time. So when a lodger 'known by the name of Jack … prevailed upon her to go off with him', she did. Yet the elopement was short-lived. Tracking his wife down, Taylor brought her home, and for the next twenty-four hours at least, they lived again as man and wife before Taylor shot her in the back.[32]

Alongside long incarcerations, as observed by Frost, the inquest reports also reveal that adultery took place between wives and lodgers during the fleeting absence of a husband. In 1894, an adulterous relationship began under William Hailes's roof at 5 Toppesfield Road, Nunhead Green, London, between Mrs Hailes and their lodger, twenty-eight-year-old carpenter George Robert Barton. It was stated that they had become intimately 'acquainted' when Mr Hailes 'was away from home for a fortnight owing to illness', presumably in the workhouse infirmary, and the affair continued after he returned. Not long after, the couple eloped.[33] Yet it is perhaps also the case that the absence of a husband provided an opportunity for a determined male seducer. In January 1894, fifty-year-old Mary Brooker's body was recovered from a pond near the home she shared with her husband, farm labourer William Brooker, in the Surrey Parish of Charlwood. A note in her handwriting found afterwards stated, 'God bless my husband and children. It is not through my husband I have done this; God forgive me, I hope.' A coroner's inquest revealed that with her husband having 'been laid up nearly a year' and with still two dependent children at home, the family lived on the support of the parish. But to supplement this, they were compelled to take in a lodger. The unknown male lodger – unnamed at the coroner's inquest – proved to be the ruin of Mary.

Various witnesses called to testify as to the state of Mary's mind at the time of her death revealed that she had been 'depressed and suicidal'. Because of this and her father's illness, Mary's elder daughter, Kate, returned home from service to assist her parents. Upon her return, she learnt of her mother's brief affair with the lodger, which she revealed to the coroner's court in her testimony: 'In July a lodger slept with her whilst her father was away for the week.' This brief but adulterous encounter 'preyed on [Mary's] mind', and she was greatly concerned that, as a result, she 'was in *enceinte*'. Indeed, Mary requested a local surgeon, Mr Sydney Philip Matthews M.R.C.S. (already attendant on Mary due to existing health issues), to examine her on several occasions for signs of pregnancy. He informed her each time 'that she was not'.[34] William Brooker omitted in the first instance to mention his wife's infidelity to the coroner. However, he was immediately recalled following his daughter's revelations to the court. Pressed by the coroner, he stated that he learnt of the relationship November last as 'She had told him so herself, and he forgave her.' Evidently, Mary was unable to carry the burden of her guilt. William further noted, 'she had been despondent ever since, and had referred to it repeatedly'.[35] Reading between the lines of this case, particularly when considering the acute mental anguish suffered by Mary due to the liaison with the unnamed male lodger, we could speculate whether the intercourse that took place was consensual. This would perhaps explain why her husband went to great lengths to conceal the affair with the lodger from the coroner's court. For if to have a wife commit adultery was to question the husband's virality and rule over home, then what would it say about him for his wife to have been raped by the lodger he had taken under his roof?

How did husbands react to a wife's adultery with the lodger? For not only had he been made a cuckold, but he had been cuckolded under *his* own roof and probably even between the sheets of *his* own bed. His reputation was damaged, his virility brought into question, and the authority over his home weakened; a response was almost expected.[36] These responses were typically violent. Of course, by their very nature, the cases of wife–lodger adultery revealed in the coroner's court are usually tied to violent reactions culminating in the killing of a spouse or lodger. Yet despite the extremes of the cases discussed below, they are also telling in the community's response to the unfaithful wife and the cuckolded husband. Taylor was one of forty-two men who were placed on trial in England for murder motivated by their wives' infidelity between 1841 and 1900.[37] Taylor freely admitted to those living under his roof – as testified at the coroner's inquest – that murder was on his mind as he tracked down his wife and lodger: 'He told me that he first thought of drowning her in the cut at Wootton Bassett, whilst on the road home, but thinking it would put her to too much punishment, he determined upon bringing her home and then shooting her.' The next day, hearing Jack – the lodger – was about the premises 'with a view of taking her off' again, he shot his wife in the back. The gun was so heavily charged, that it burst into several pieces.'

The community's response to Hannah Taylor's murder was unequivocal. Despite clear evidence of adultery, neighbours attested to the local press that 'up to the time of her acquaintance with the railway man [Jack], [Hannah] bore a good character'. On the other hand, her husband was seen as an ungodly man: 'he was never seen but once at church'. Following an accident whereby his arm became infected, the family surgeon:

> found him cursing and swearing, and using the most blasphemous language. Upon being remonstrated with, and told that he should

pray ... he replied – that he had prayed for the whole of the last week, and got worse: and he was going to try what a week's cursing would do! ... It is even said, that whilst his aged father was lying on his death-bed, he attempted to set the house on fire. He frequently carried a gun, and was in the habit of threatening to shoot different persons, and was consequently the terror of the neighbourhood.

Nor was he a remorseful man, telling the coroner's court that 'Twas I that killed my wife and no one else, and I am glad of it.' Notwithstanding, the press report surmised 'that he was "dotingly fond of his wife" [and] he had suffered in body and mind from her infidelity'. To the surprise of the coroner, who endeavoured, in the circumstances of adultery, to sway the jury toward a manslaughter verdict, the jury – entirely intertwined with the community it served and therefore acquainted with Taylor's reputation – was unequivocal in their verdict, for 'without a moment's hesitation, returned a verdict of WILFUL MURDER against James Taylor'.[38]

However, the issue of provocation played out somewhat differently in the criminal court proceedings. Sent to the assize for trial, Taylor pleaded not guilty to wilful murder. He now claimed that in preparing his gun to shoot his wife's lover, it accidentally went off and killed his wife. Notably, he did not deny the intent to kill, just – in the eyes of the law, as will be examined below – a more justifiable homicide. In this case, the assize jury – less acquainted with Taylor – found Taylor guilty but recommended the prisoner for mercy because of his wife's adultery. After all, the provocation defence spared many men the death sentence for killing their wives.[39] However, Mr Justice Erskine did not heed the jury's plea to spare Taylor's life. Donning his black cap, Erskine acknowledged that while the crime was committed under provocation and that, indeed, his wife was guilty of adultery, 'the law does not acknowledge [this] as affording any extension for your crime'. In Erskine's view, Taylor's actions were carried out 'in the most deliberate manner', and his wife's unfaithfulness, he concluded, did 'not authorise [him] to take her life'.[40]

A lodger's life, however, was an entirely different matter. As opposed to having killed an unfaithful wife, Martin Wiener found that 'doing violence' or even killing a wife's lover when adultery had been proven 'was normally treated with some indulgence'.[41] This was certainly the case when it came to lodgers. On the night of

29 December 1895, in the colliery village of Standish, near Wigan, farm labourer Joseph Ellis Jones, after a night of drinking, killed Michael McDonough – his lodger – in the back kitchen of his home. Jones claimed that he had acted in self-defence – that McDonough, otherwise known as Burke, had 'attempted to hit him with a poker, but he wrestled it from him and gave him "a crack or two" on the head, after which he went to bed, leaving [McDonough] sleeping on the hearthrug … he did not know he had killed [him], and did not intend to do so'. Cracks began to appear in Jones' account when the silent witness, McDonough's body, revealed he had been strangled. Arising from this were questions of motive, with 'whisper[ings] that jealously is not altogether dissociated from the crime'. McDonough, it was believed, was having adulterous relations with Jones's wife. After a five-hour inquest and 'a prolonged deliberation', questioning whether Jones's actions had been premeditated, the coroner's jury returned a verdict of manslaughter.[42]

At the Assize trial, the seduction of Jones's wife by the lodger played a crucial role in the defence. If they could prove provocation, then they could sway the jury. Neighbours – the ever-watchful force in working-class communities – and Jones's workmates were called to provide testimony of the adultery. Elizabeth Banford and Ellen Preston – 'two married women' – had informed Jones that McDonough was 'too thick' with Mrs Jones. The revelation of this preyed on Jones's mind, as revealed in the testimony of farm bailiff Thomas Hilton: 'Three weeks before Christmas [I] came across Jones, who was leaning with his head in his hands. [I] asked what was the matter. Jones replied that he was a little bit upset in his mind. "Why?" … "I don't like what is going on between lodger and my missus." [I] told him not to mind, as lodgers would joke. Jones, however, said that "this is above a joke."' Jones's wife, away at the time of her lodger's killing, was not called to testify as to whether the claimed adultery had taken place or not. Nonetheless, there was no question that McDonough had died at the hand of Jones, and the jury, 'after a few minutes deliberation', found Jones guilty of manslaughter. Concurring with the defence, 'they added that [Jones] had committed the crime under great provocation'. In other words, the jury believed that the lodger had been, to some extent, responsible for his death. While such a line of defence was falling out of favour by the time of Jones's trial, this had some sway with the judge, Mr

Justice Vaughan Williams, who sentenced Jones to just three months hard labour.[43]

Some husbands with a hand in their lodger's demise did not even get as far as criminal proceedings. After two weeks of searching for his wife and former lodger, William Hailes located them in lodgings – as discussed in Chapter 2, a convenient domestic arrangement for eloping couples – on the Old Kent Road. Forcibly entering the house and confronting Barton, Hailes declared, '"I have found you at last, you — monkey," and then violently kicked him in the stomach'. Barton managed to escape, but the following week, Barton, arriving at his brother's house, complained of pains resulting from the kick, fell downstairs and, being severely injured, was conveyed to the hospital, where he later died. Examining the details of the case, the coroner's jury – undoubtedly considering the wrong that Barton had done to Hailes – did not hold Hailes accountable for Barton's demise and returned a verdict of accidental death.[44] There would be no criminal trial.

For some men, the humiliation of their wives' adultery was too much of a burden to bear. If they could not reassert mastery over their home, they – as Lawrence Stone observed – became the joke of the village.[45] Humiliated by his wife's elopement with their lodger just months into their marriage, twenty-three-year-old Jasper Wells drowned himself in a water tank. The suicide note revealed, conversely, that it was not his wife's adultery directly that led him to suicide, but rather the response of the community: 'he could stand no longer the taunts of his fellow men with regards to the conduct of his wife', and thus saw no other action but to take his own life.[46]

Happy endings?

By their very nature, coroners' inquests are skewed towards presenting cases of disastrous marriages and cohabitations between female householders and their lodgers; most, as noted above, involve the suicide or murder of at least one of the partners involved. Beyond the confines of the coroner's courts, however, there were undoubtedly enduring (if not happy) unions whose beginnings of which were formed in the householder–lodger relationship. Having survived an attempt on her life by her first lodger-turned-husband,

Mary Burdock née Sloper went on to marry another of her lodgers – coachbuilder Henry Balkwell – in a marriage that lasted for twenty years, and one where there was little necessity for a lodger.[47] Others lived in adulterous cohabitation or, even when they could wed, lived together as man and wife. Jessie Wells was married to her husband Jasper Wells just a few months before eloping with their lodger, agricultural labourer Albert Sands. This second union proved more successful, though initially lacking any legal union. As noted above, Jessie and Albert had been free to marry within months of their elopement, after Jessie's husband died by suicide.[48] Albert and Jessie even presented themselves as married and, as was the case among many working-class cohabiting couples, likely saw themselves as so. They even had two children, registering both as the legitimate children of Albert.[49] Yet Albert and Jessie did not wed for another fourteen years. Despite presenting himself as a bachelor on his wedding day, Albert may well have been bound to another until this time. Whether this was the case or not, the couple had remained together for forty-nine years before Albert died in 1943.

Conclusion

Played out in the Victorian coroner's courts, widows, wives, and their lodgers do not follow the scripts that have long shaped our understanding of the boundaries crossed in these relationships. Widows were far from the husband hunters praying upon unsuspecting lodgers. Instead, these were women in crisis, endeavouring to maintain their homes and families without the male breadwinner wage. So when they received the attention of a lodger, they might well consider his proposition of courtship to alleviate their struggle. But, as Betty Scott's case illustrates, widows were not necessarily in a hurry to wed the male lodgers with whom they had established a courtship, their position as head of the household permitting them the power to be choosy. Yet where the lodger remained in limbo – not quite lodger, not quite husband, because the woman with whom he lodged would not or could not marry – complex power dynamics came into play. This often resulted in a burgeoning jealousy tipping into violence from their lack of authority in *her* home. In the end, the paramour lodger's only power was through violence, which, when the courtships ended and he had been served notice to leave, came to a tragic conclusion.

The presence of lodgers in the marital home, as I show in Chapter 1, was ubiquitous in Victorian working-class society. It is safe to say that most wives – at the first opportunity – did not jump into bed with their male lodgers, as perhaps Victorian music hall had led us to believe. Nonetheless, the male lodger's presence – signalling the male breadwinner's failure to provide for his family – could cause domestic discord where instability already existed. Sensing a loss of authority over *his* home, a husband could harbour unfounded jealousy that led to the most heinous crimes. Yet, in some cases, the coroner's inquests do confirm cases of adultery between wives and lodgers. Left with their homes in disarray, working-class husbands sought retribution. This, of course, could not be found through the divorce courts, a cost beyond the working man's pocket. Instead, cuckolded husbands took matters into their own hands. Yet it mattered how they handled it, not only, most significantly, to those who suffered and died at their hands, but it also determined the likelihood of their punishment. Taking the life of an unfaithful wife could be harshly punished, albeit with provocation taken into account, but to take the life of a lodger – someone they had trusted enough to take under their roof – was an entirely different matter. In the Victorian (coroner and criminal) courts, the lodger as a matter of course was guilty of provocation.

Notes

1 For more information on the fictional portrayals of widows in the Victorian period, see Nadine Muller, 'Desperately Funny: Victorian Widows & the Comical Misfortunes of Husband Hunting', *Journal of Gender Studies*, 29:8 (2020), 926–36. DOI: 10.1080/0958923 6.2020.1819777.
2 Muller, 'Desperately Funny', 930.
3 Muller, 'Desperately Funny', 930.
4 *Burnley Express*, 7 January 1882, p. 8; *Burnley Express*, 18 February 1882, p. 6.
5 Leonore Davidoff, 'The Separation of Home and Work? Landladies and Lodgers in Nineteenth-and Twentieth-Century England', in Sandra Burman (ed.), *Fit Work for Women* (London: Croom Helm, 1979), pp. 89–91; Megan Doolittle, Janet Fink, and Katherine Holden, *The Family*

Story: *Blood, Contract, and Intimacy, 1830–1960* (London: Longman, 1999), p. 181. Many thanks to Gillian Williamson for sharing her postcard collection with me.
6 Ginger S. Frost, *Living in Sin: Cohabiting as Husband and Wife in Nineteenth-Century England* (Manchester: Manchester University Press, 2011), pp. 97, 109, 112, 116.
7 Vicky Holmes, *In Bed with the Victorians: The Life-Cycle of Working-Class Marriage* (Cham: Springer Nature, 2017), Chapter 5. The case involved a man who, on separating from his wife, took up lodgings with an elderly widow. According to him, they soon began to live as man and wife despite her being many years his senior. However, whatever the true nature of the relationship, witness testimonies at the inquest into the widow's death (determined to be from natural causes) revealed the relationship was abusive and disguised from her children.
8 Julie-Marie Strange, *Death, Grief, and Poverty in Britain 1870–1914* (Cambridge: Cambridge University Press, 2010), p. 196.
9 Strange, *Death, Grief, and Poverty*, p. 197.
10 Muller, 'Desperately Funny', 926–36.
11 Betty's husband died in late 1868, and she appears to have been in receipt of outdoor relief until the point of her death in 1882 (having been in a relationship with Templeton in the preceding months).
12 Pat Thane, 'Women and the Poor Law in Victorian and Edwardian England', *History Workshop*, 6 (1978), 40.
13 Frost, *Living in Sin*, pp. 128–9.
14 Frost, *Living in Sin*, p. 128.
15 *Burnley Express*, 7 January 1882, p. 6; *Burnley Gazette*, 28 January 1882, p. 6; Frost, *Living in Sin*, pp. 34, 39, 117, 132.
16 Frost, *Living in Sin*, pp. 96–118, 123–43.
17 Frost, *Living in Sin*, p. 108.
18 *Burnley Express*, 13 June 1894, p. 3; *Burnley Express*, 16 June 1894, p. 8; *Burnley Express*, 4 July 1894, p. 3. In Carolyn A. Conley's work on judges and jurors in criminal courts, she argues that the level of direction given by a judge varied widely depending on their perception of jurors' abilities. Carolyn A. Conley, *The Unwritten Law: Criminal Justice in Victorian Kent* (Oxford: Oxford University Press, 1991), p. 16.
19 *Manchester Evening News*, 12 July 1894, pp. 2–3; *Burnley Express*, 21 July 1894, p. 6.
20 *Bristol Mercury*, 7 November 1846, p. 2; *Bristol Mercury*, 10 April 1847, p. 4. While employed in someone's house, Ferris attempted to kill a man, claiming he had wronged her. Sentenced to death, Louisa died in the Hobart prison hospital before her execution. *The Cornwall*

Chronicle (Tasmania), 28 April 1852, pp. 277–8; *The Courier* (Tasmania), 3 March 1854, p. 2.

21 The confusion over the status of their relationship ran over into numerous accounts of the inquest reported across the country, for this woman's death and the ambiguity over her domestic arrangements gained national interest. Some reports describe Lloyd as 'a lodger', others as her 'paramour', while another stated they 'cohabited as man and wife'. *Birmingham Post*, 17 January 1894, p. 7; *Yorkshire Evening Post*, 15 January 1894, p. 3; *Lincolnshire Echo*, 15 January 1894, p. 3; *Gloucestershire Citizen*, 15 January 1894, p. 3.

22 *Walsall Observer*, 20 January 1894, p. 3; *Walsall Observer*, 17 March 1894, p. 2; *Birmingham Post*, 12 March 1894, p. 5.

23 Davidoff, 'The Separation of Home and Work', p. 91; also see Leonore Davidoff, *Worlds Between: Historical Perspectives on Gender and Class* (Cambridge: Polity Press, 1995), p. 173.

24 For more information on why working-class women remained in 'bad' marriages, see Holmes, *In Bed with the Victorians*, p. 58.

25 Robert Roberts, *A Ragged Schooling* (Harmondsworth: Penguin, 1997) p. 89.

26 Confessing immediately after the act, he spent the rest of his days in Broadmoor, dying in 1903 at the age of fifty. *Birmingham Mail*, 26 June 1876, p. 3; *Birmingham & Aston Chronicle*, 1 July 1 1876, p. 5; *Aris's Birmingham Gazette*, 14 October 1876, p. 6; *Birmingham Daily Post*, 7 December 1876, p. 6; *Leamington Spa Courier*, 9 December 1876, p. 7; *Birmingham Daily Post*, 9 January 1877, p. 6.

27 *Newcastle Journal*, 8 March 1870, p. 3. *Bradford Daily Telegraph*, 8 March 1870, p. 4; *Shields Gazette & Daily Telegraph*, 8 March 1870, p. 4; *Newcastle Courant*, 11 March 1870, p. 2.

28 Robert Roberts, *A Ragged Schooling* (Harmondsworth: Penguin, 1978) p. 82, cited in Davidoff, 'The Separation of Home and Work', pp. 90–1.

29 A search of 'lodger AND elopement' between 1850 and 1899 in *The British Newspaper Archive* yields 16,034 results.

30 *Maidstone Journal and Kentish Advertiser*, 31 May 1894, p. 6; *Bromley and District Times*, 25 May 1894, p. 5.

31 *Royal Cornwall Gazette*, 17 July 1840, p. 2.

32 *Devizes and Wiltshire Gazette*, 9 July 1840, p. 3.

33 *South London Press*, 12 May 1894, p. 5.

34 *Sussex Agricultural Express*, 23 January 1894, p. 3.

35 *Sussex Agricultural Express*, 23 January 1894, p. 3.

36 Lawrence Stone, *The Family, Sex and Marriage in England 1500–1800* (London: Weidenfeld & Nicolson, 1977), pp. 316–17.

37 And, as Wiener notes, at least a further twenty-three had been moti-vated by an 'unsubstantiated belief in his wife's infidelity'. Martin J. Wiener, *Men of Blood: Violence, Manliness, and Criminal Justice in Victorian England* (Cambridge: Cambridge University Press, 2006), p. 201.

38 *Devizes and Wiltshire Gazette*, 9 July 1840, p. 3.

39 For more information on the adultery provocation defence in murder cases in the Victorian period, see Wiener, *Men of Blood*, pp. 201–39; K. J. Kesselring, 'No Greater Provocation? Adultery and the Mitigation of Murder in English Law', *Law and History Review*, 34:1 (2016), 199–225. DOI: 10.1017/S0738248015000681.

40 *Devizes and Wiltshire Gazette*, 4 March 1841, p. 3.

41 Wiener, *Men of Blood*, p. 202.

42 *Blackburn Standard*, 4 January 1896, p. 2; *South Wales Echo*, 2 January 1896, p. 2.

43 *Bolton Evening News*, 28 February 1896, p. 3; *Manchester Courier*, 29 February 1896, p. 9.

44 *South London Press*, 12 May 1894, p. 5; sometimes referred to as 'Ayles'.

45 As Lawrence Stone states, 'the honour of a married man was severely damaged if he got the reputation of being a cuckold since this was a slur on both his virility and his capacity to rule his own household. He became the joke of the village.' Stone, *The Family, Sex and Marriage*, pp. 316–17.

46 *Maidstone Journal and Kentish Advertiser*, 31 May 1894, p. 6; *Bromley and District Times*, 25 May 1894, p. 5.

47 Lodgers are neither present in the 1901 nor 1911 census, where Mary Balkwell is listed as a housewife. TNA, RG13/1385, f. 58, p. 13, s. 105, 1901 England, Wales & Scotland Census; TNA, RG14/8148, s. 157, 1911 England, Wales & Scotland Census.

48 *Maidstone Journal and Kentish Advertiser*, 31 May 1894, p. 6; *Bromley and District Times*, 25 May 1894, p. 5.

49 Tracing the couple's story, we discover that, while still living with her husband, Jessie had fallen pregnant with Sands's child – the likely cata-lyst for their elopement. By 1901, the couple, having moved around several locations in Kent (evidenced by their children's place of birth), were living on the Isle of Sheppey as man and wife. Notably, despite being unmarried at this point, they had registered their two daughters as the legitimate daughters of Sands and informed the census enumera-tor that they were a married couple. TNA, RG13/818, f. 32, p. 4, s. 4, 1901 England, Wales & Scotland Census.

6

Notice to quit

When in May 1864, twenty-one-year-old policeman William Antcliffe took lodgings in the Lincolnshire home of shepherd William Vickers and his wife Ann, they found him to be the ideal lodger. As Ann revealed to the coroner's court investigating her young lodger's death three months later, 'He has always conducted himself well; was not given to intoxication at all; and was always steady and attentive.' Moreover, he always paid up what he owed for his board and monthly lodgings.[1] Even after consuming poison with the intent to take his own life for reasons the coroner's inquest could not determine, Antcliffe paid for what was owed in board and lodgings: 'He jumped off the bed, and paid me £2 10s; he owed me £2 5s. for his board and lodgings. He shook hands with me, and said he would not die in debt.' Despite the efforts of the surgeon called by the Vickers, their lodger's life could not be saved.[2]

Few domestic dwelling lodgings arrangements would have come to such a dramatic end as that which occurred under the Vickers' roof in 1864. Yet without such tragic occurrences, matters regarding the end of the domestic dwelling lodging arrangements would largely evade historical records. Indeed, except for Gillian Williamson's work on eighteenth-century lodgings, little is known about how the householder–lodger relationships came to a close.[3] In the reading of these misfortunes detailed in the inquest reports, we not only find details regarding the more extreme ends to the lodging arrangement but also locate the more typical circumstances that led lodgers to move on from their domestic dwelling lodgings or for householders to cease taking in lodgers. Furthermore, going against the assumption of the informalities of the domestic dwelling lodgings arrangement, I also demonstrate in this chapter that while not always a written process, the working-class householder generally lived within the letter of the law when removing unwanted lodgers from their home, even if their lodgers did not.

Notice to quit

Serving notice to quit was an expectation on both sides of the lodging exchange. When the time came to move on, whether heading off to marry or to seek more congenial lodgings, most lodgers undoubtedly gave sufficient notice – i.e. a week if lodging had been taken by the week – and settled any outstanding arrears.[4] Few inquest reports hint at the emotional strain of a lodger's departure, but we can speculate that where relationships had been harmonious, the departure was tinged with sadness. Elizabeth Hendreys, for example, was noted to have 'been desponding in her mind relative to the departure from her house' a lodger who had been with them for eight years.[5] Overwhelmingly, however, when it comes to moving on, the inquest reports tend to signal a relief in the termination of the relationship.

The inconsiderate lodger might depart their lodgings without notice, leaving behind any arrears they have accrued for board and lodgings. As seen in Chapter 3, householders could, through distress for rent, detain their lodger's goods to recoup what was owed. However, once a lodger was no longer living under their roof, any arrears became a debt that, by law, had to be claimed through the courts. Long, drawn-out, costly court proceedings were a last resort for working-class householders. Less-than-honest lodgers would have been well aware of this matter.[6] Therefore, when Sabina Foy, wife of Islington labourer Thomas Foy, discovered her lodger was planning on removing without having paid rent owed, she 'endeavour[ed] to detain some of the lodger's goods' before that rent owed became a debt claimable only through the courts. Unsurprisingly, some householders faced resistance when attempting to seize their lodger's possessions, whether done by the book or not. When neighbour William Cole came 'to help the [lodger] take away her goods', the Foys – threatened with violence – could do little to prevent him. Indeed, with tensions flared, the following day, Thomas Foy and Cole engaged in a fight that was to prove fatal.[7] Meanwhile, undoubtedly lacking the means to pursue her recently departed lodger's debt through the courts, seventy-three-year-old Hannah Newton took to her feet to recoup what was owed. Despite her ailing health, Newton travelled by foot from her home in Chapeltown to Holmfield – a five-mile round trip – to find her lodger and call up the debt. Whether Newton got her money, we do not know. What we do know, however, is that the journey – as she had herself predicted to a neighbour – proved to be the death of her. Two days following her excursion, Newton was found dead by her bedside.[8]

Lodgers in persistent arrears and unwilling to address the unpaid sums would generally find themselves served notice to quit by an exasperated householder. After all, as observed in Chapter 1, among the working class, lodgers were generally taken in to alleviate financial distress and, in not paying their dues, could place significant strain on already struggling households. While some might cast a lodger out at a moment's notice, the inquest reports suggest that householders generally followed the necessary protocol. Bound to the same law between landlords and tenants, householders appear to have typically served the required notice to quit even in the most strained circumstances. For example, when twenty-eight-year-old John Neillan and his wife, Susan, took up lodgings in the Stockon-on-Tees home of brickmaker John Brannan, they paid for their board and lodgings 'pretty regularly for some time'. Yet just a few months later, the Neillans got into arrears and – according to the Brannans – showed no 'inclination to overtake them'. Arriving home one evening, determined to address the issue of non-payment, John Brannan 'inquired of his wife whether the lodgers had paid for their board and lodgings, and also whether they had paid certain arrears which were owing on that account. Mrs Brannan replied they had not, and her husband informed Neillan and his wife they would have to quit the house.' After all, a failure to pay the agreed rent was a breach of the lodging contract, verbal or not. A quarrel ensued, with John Brannan being violently struck by Susan and John Neillan. After the row subsided, the Neillans agreed to settle their debts. Providing the Brannans with a sovereign and a 'quantity of articles as security for the balance', they did not remain for the notice period but took immediate leave of their lodgings.[9]

However, notice to quit was not just served upon financially irksome lodgers. Where lodgers might bring 'respectable' working-class homes into disrepute, householders were prompt in pursuing their removal. For example, in Chapter 2, we saw married women given notice to quit when it was discovered that the men with whom they arrived were not their husbands.[10] Disruptive lodgers who made life difficult for the householder and their fellow lodgers were also promptly served notice to quit. As so many working-class householders – particularly those headed by females – depended on the income from more than one lodger, disruptive lodgers needed to be removed before their more reliable fellow lodgers decided to move on. One of the compelling reasons Mrs Mary Ann Allen – whom we have already met several times – served her paramour-lodger notice to leave after the breakdown of their intimate relationship was the fear that she would lose her other lodgers because of his behaviour: 'I am not going to have my house emptied for the sake of you.'[11]

Notice served for disruptive behaviour was not just confined to lodgers who were once lovers. On arriving in the Yorkshire town of Hemsworth, fifty-four-year-old draper's traveller George Stamper took up lodgings in the home of miner Solomon Harper and his wife, Elizabeth. However, Stamper's time under their roof was short-lived. Six weeks after his arrival, Stamper's heavy drinking caused him to lose both his employment and lodgings. Giving evidence at an inquest held following Stamper's body being pulled from the River Dearne, Elizabeth Harper stated she 'had given him notice to leave, on account of his disturbing the other lodgers at night'.[12] Meanwhile, narrowly avoiding being the subject of a coroner's inquest, widow Elizabeth Cooper survived a brutal attack by one of her lodgers, twenty-five-year-old Harry Slaughter. Cooper had given Slaughter notice 'on the grounds that he was quarrelsome when under the influence of drink, and had challenged her son to a fight'. Responding to the notice to quit Cooper's home, Slaughter was heard to say, 'I shall do something very bad before I leave this house.' Like William Crossley and Robert Templeton in Chapter 5, Slaughter, by law, could remain in his lodgings during the notice period, allowing him to avenge what he saw as a slight on his person. Two days after being served notice, while Cooper was making the beds, Slaughter 'jumped out of his bed and attacked her with a razor'.[13]

However, serving notice to leave did not necessarily lead to a lodger's departure. If a lodger refused to accept the notice, there was little legal recourse to remove them.[14] Laundress Jane Carnell committed several crimes that found her frequently before Exeter's Police Court.[15] Following her final prison sentence, Carnell lodged in the home of Jane Pinn. Yet Carnell soon owed money to Pinn for rent, 'some money she had lent her, and some goods'. Eventually, Pinn served Carnell notice to quit, though this was not because of the increasing amount of money owed. Instead, Carnell was served notice on account of her annoying Pinn's other lodgers – it was noted she was 'a very violent woman, and she drank'. Yet Carnell 'refused' to accept the notice, and Pinn 'could not get her out of the house'. As discussed in Chapter 4, only when Carnell stole from a fellow lodger did she finally exit from Pinn's home, although in a coffin rather than on her own two feet, for Carnell died by suicide when the victim threatened to report the theft to the police.[16]

Even the police could not intervene to remove a troublesome and potentially dangerous lodger. When shoemaker Thomas Walker and his wife took up lodgings in the Hackney home of harness maker James Whitton, it soon became apparent they would be difficult lodgers and that getting them out of their home would be impossible.[17] Not long after the Walkers' arrival, 'words' were exchanged between Mrs Walker and Mrs Whitton, leading to a festering contempt between the two women that soon led to violence: 'On the Saturday morning Mrs Walker came into the kitchen, and insulted [Mrs Whitton] by throwing a pail of water over her head.' After a further exchange of words, Whitton 'struck' her lodger. That evening, Mr Walker was informed by the Whittons that 'You must find another place for your wife, for she is a dangerous one.' Outraged at the slur, Mrs Walker 'spat' in Whitton's face and declared, 'I'll leave when I like.' The Whittons, perhaps trusting that a written rather than verbal notice would hold more authority, handed Thomas Walker a written notice to quit. However, the letter merely served to fuel the fire. After an evening of drinking, the Walkers returned to their lodgings in the early hours, directing 'beastly language' at the Whittons as they made their way to bed.

The following day, on remonstrating with his troublesome lodgers, James Whitton was challenged to a fight by Thomas Walker. Brushing off the request, James Whitton returned downstairs to the room below the Walkers to find a 'perfect pour' of water coming through the floor of Walker's room. Calling in the police in the hope that they might be able to remove the Walkers, they found that while the police expressed the opinion that Walker was 'a rascal that ought to be punished', they did not have the power to remove them. Moments after the police departed, Thomas Walker pushed Mrs Whitton out of the back passage and into the yard, '[striking] her on the nose with his fist'. Screaming for her husband, who ran to her aide, he was seized by Walker, who 'struck him unmercifully about the head with a salt box'. Believing the lodger intended to kill her husband, Mrs Whitton 'seized a tin can and struck Walker about the head' before she and her husband fled to the parlour and locked the door behind them. While the lock might prevent access to the light-fingered lodger, the door itself could not withstand the brute force of an enraged lodger, with Walker 'kick[ing] at the door until he broke the panel in'. Convinced that his lodger meant to murder him, James Whitton jumped out of the window to get help. However, Whitton 'overbalanced and fell [and] was picked up dead'. At the ensuing coroner's inquest, steering the jury, the coroner, Mr Richards, stated 'that the case was clearly one of manslaughter. The deceased, while trying to escape from the illegal violence of the accused, and while labouring under the fear of being murdered, had lost his life.' As we have seen, such a steer from the coroner was not entirely unusual, and 'after a short consultation', the jury returned a verdict of manslaughter. A warrant for Thomas Walker's arrest was issued, whereby he was charged with 'feloniously killing and slaying his landlord' and sent to Newgate to await trial, a trial in which he was found not guilty, for the Old Bailey jury determined that the fall had not been the cause of death, thus exonerating Walker.[18]

Perhaps those who had the most authority to remove a lodger from domestic dwelling lodgings were the Poor Law authorities. Sick and elderly lodgers placed both a significant financial and domestic burden upon the householders accommodating them. Where they lacked a familial safety net, householders encouraged such lodgers to turn to the workhouse when they could no longer pay their rent. In her fifties, Great Bolton weaver Hannah Lomax found her health deteriorating and, struggling to earn little more than 2s. 8d. a week, 'The person with whom she lodged advised her to go to the workhouse, as there was no other prospect for her.' However, such

was her dread of entering the workhouse, Hannah drowned herself
– the coroner's jury determined – 'whilst in a state of temporary
insanity, caused *by want*'.[19] Some, however, did make it through the
workhouse doors. As seen in Chapter 2, bachelor Adam Robinson,
having never settled in lodgings for any great length of time, ended
his days in Burnley's workhouse.[20]

Other householders were prompt to seek out the assistance of
the relieving officers to remove such lodgers. Yet even here, some
householders struggled to remove those who burdened them significantly. Harriet Eliza Pollard, aged sixty-two years, had boarded
and lodged in the Weston-Super-Mare home of Miss Eliza Chandler
for almost two decades. During this time, Harriet had been in good
health, but in her final year under Chandler's roof, she 'began to
have delusions of a religious nature'. Chandler promptly took her
to Dr Roxburgh, who 'prescribed for her'. However, in the following months, Harriet became increasingly 'strange in her manners
and habits, also very dirty'. She also began to refuse food. Chandler
attempted 'to feed her', but more often than not, Harriet 'threw the
food into the fire, and out of the window'. Struggling to care for
her lodger, Chandler wrote to a relative to inform him of the situation and seek advice: 'He said the only way out of the difficulty
would be to send her to the Asylum, and the way to do it would
be to apply to the relieving officer', which she did. However, Mr
Hitchen, the parish doctor, on assessing Harriet, determined that
she was 'a perfectly harmless lunatic, and not at all a fit case for the
asylum. Considering that she would be well taken care of where
she was [with Chandler], he did not feel justified in signing a cer-
tificate' – a position he maintained even as Harriet's situation deteriorated. Harriet took to being 'very noisy, particularly at night',
causing complaints from Chandler's neighbours. In her final weeks
in Chandler's home, Harriet developed bed sores and became 'quite
unmanageable'. Chandler tried to treat the bed sores, 'but [Harriet]
would not let me put anything on them. Her strength was such
that I could not manage her.' Chandler herself, at this point, was
in her late fifties. 'Determined to send her to the asylum', Chandler
sent for Dr Roxburgh, who, along with a local magistrate, certi-
fied Hannah's removal. Arranging a cab, Chandler herself took her
lodger to the asylum. When admitted, Hannah weighed just three
stone.[21]

Some lodgers, however, died peacefully in their lodgings, tended to by the women with whom they lodged. Long-term lodger John Hampson, for example, having lodged with the same family for several decades, died under the roof of Edna Prescott – the woman with whom he lodged and the daughter of the woman with whom he had previously lodged.[22] Thirty-two-year-old destitute widow Deborah Willis was not turned out by the woman with whom she lodged – Julia Toler – who herself was in strained circumstances. Toler had 'recommended' that Willis 'should go to the Union', but when Willis objected, Toler continued to provide bed and board without seeing a penny from her dying lodger. Moreover, of her 'own accord', Toler sought a doctor to tend to Willis and was the one who administered the prescribed draught 'every four hours'. When Willis died in the night on a bed made of a sack of shavings, she was not alone. '[Toler] was present when she died.'[23]

Till death do us part

Death was a frequent dismantler of the lodging arrangement. For lodgers, the death of the householder meant packing up what belongings they had and heading off in search of new lodgings, just as Adam Robinson and Robert Chadwick did – together – following the murder of Mrs Mary Ann Allen. Even perpetual lodgers could find themselves moving on more than once in their lifetime on account of the death of the women with whom they lodged. Of course, new lodgings could be promptly found within the local community, as seen in Chapter 3, so a sudden and unexpected move would not have extensively inconvenienced lodgers. Yet this is not to say that lodgers were unaffected by the death of the householder, especially when a bond between lodger and householder had been forged over the years. For seventy-three-year-old retired Cornish farmer Richard James, the death of the woman with whom he had lodged for three or four years – a Mrs Aver – appears to have been the final straw that drove him to die by suicide. Mrs Edwards, called to testify at the coroner's inquest into James's death, stated that after Aver's death, James continued to 'sle[ep] in his own room in the empty house' while she, being local to James, now provided his food. However, with his time in the house expiring and 'very much put out', James was meant to take up lodgings with a neighbouring farmer but, evidently not wanting to leave the home to which he had become accustomed, took his own life.[24]

For some women who lodged with married couples, the death of the female householder provided them an opportunity. We do not know why or exactly when Ann Ley and her husband, Morris, separated. Living together in Bristol in 1851, Morris was employed as a plasterer and was the breadwinner of a marriage lasting thus far twelve years.[25] After this point, there is a twenty-year gap in the records regarding this couple. By the night of the 1871 census, Ann – now aged fifty-seven, living apart from her husband, and reporting her occupation as a nurse – was living on Tankard Close as a lodger in the home of cordwainer James McGuire and his wife Hannah, alongside another female lodger and two male lodgers.[26] Shortly after Ann arrived at the McGuire's home, Hannah died, providing Ann with the opportunity to establish a more permanent footing in the house. Ley was no longer a lodger but the woman who 'kept house' for the widowed James McGuire.[27]

The death of a lodger could also have far-reaching consequences on the householder. While householders were, in theory, able to chase the debts of lodgers who had departed their homes on their own two feet, there was little or no recourse for those whose lodgers had died unexpectedly. Having travelled from his native Switzerland to London in 1886, thirty-three-year-old tailor John Buchler took up lodgings in the Wardour Street home of German hairdresser A. Schoenleben. For two years, Buchler lodged under their roof before one day heading out to Plumstead, where he was later found hanging in a cattle shed. At the inquest, Schoenleben, testifying as to his lodger's state of mind, revealed that Buchler had 'got in low spirits on account of being unable to find employment'. Buchler had been out of work for four weeks and could not pay for his food and lodgings. However, rather than serve notice on his lodger, Schoenleben continued to provide food and accommodation and even loaned money to his struggling lodger, with whom he likely shared a language and a culture. Within weeks, Buchler owed Schoenleben £5 11s., a debt he did not or rather could not settle before taking his own life.[28] While not owing as significant a sum as that built up by Buchler, Birmingham widow Elizabeth Rowland's lodger – seventy-year-old shoemaker William Allman – though only briefly under her roof, 'had not paid her for what he had in her house'. Just days after his arrival, Allman went out and never returned. He had not, however, done a moonlight flit, for he had left both his shoemaker's tools and clothes in Rowland's house. A few weeks later, his body was pulled from the river.[29] We can only speculate whether Schoenleben and Rowland, following the coroner's inquests into their respective lodger's deaths, took the opportunity to sell whatever possessions left behind by their lodgers to recoup some of the money owed.

Some householders also ceased taking in lodgers following the death of a lodger, though this was not because they were financially secure. This was particularly the case where it had been the death of a long-term lodger. As noted in Chapter 3, John Last had lodged in the Vincents' Ipswich home for fourteen years. He was, by all accounts and despite the violence he enacted on Mrs Vincent, the Vincents' most dependable form of income as they slipped deeper into poverty. Whether the Vincents decided to no longer take a lodger into their home when Last died in 1894 or simply could not find a lodger for the drafty closet room slept in by Last is not recorded. Their struggle with poverty, however, can be found in the records. Following Last's death in 1894, Robert Vincent, unable to earn enough to support his family due to his health, stole food on at least one known occasion to feed his hungry family. At other times, 'a kind neighbour' had put food on their table.[30] Despite his wife's and daughter's labours, without the income from a lodger, Robert Vincent – in his fifties – surrendered to the workhouse.[31]

We first met Eliza Leaver in Chapter 1 when she and her husband moved to the bigger house in Oxford to take in lodgers to support them in old age. However, as we know, soon after that move, her husband died, and Eliza was left with a pittance for an income from three ageing male lodgers, along with a little outdoor relief. One lodger, a blind man named Hedges, who had 1s. 6d. a week in outdoor relief, earned a little by blowing the bellows at Queen's College Chapel, and had some help from some of his relations, appears to have been Leaver's primary source of income, for when he died, Eliza 'could no longer pay the big rent' on the house intended to provide her with financial stability in old age and had to give it up, for the Poor Law guardians would no longer provide her with outdoor relief if she could not earn sufficient through her own means. Faced with the prospect of having to enter the workhouse,

Eliza went into lodgings herself, and there she died in poverty.[32] In similar circumstances, when Droitwich widow Jane Hale's most reliable lodger, a man 'who had lodged in her house for some time, died', Hale 'lost the chief source of her livelihood'. Consequently, Hale decided to sell her things and move on, though exactly where she planned on going is unclear.[33]

Conclusion

As Williamson states, moving on from lodgings or ejecting lodgers was 'a natural consequence of the flexibility of lodging',[34] with lodgers moving on to marry and establish homes or simply seek more suitable accommodations. Meanwhile, alongside no longer requiring income from a lodger, householders generally desired the exit of financially or domestically troublesome lodgers. Yet despite the flexibility, there were clear expectations surrounding the termination of lodgings. Regardless of events, both parties, lodgers and householders, were expected to serve notice, which was done either verbally or – perhaps to stamp more authority on the part of the householder or in the hope to avoid confrontation – in writing. But as with all domestic arrangements, matters did not always go to plan. Attempting to avoid paying what they owed by doing a moonlight flit rather than giving notice or simply dying before they could pay up their arrears, lodgers could leave already struggling households significantly out of pocket and with little means to address the debt.

Furthermore, accounts of notice given to lodgers in the inquest reports highlight an interesting power dynamic in householder–lodger relationships. While lodgers are typically seen as the vulnerable party in the householder–lodger relationship, by the Victorian period, they appeared to have had the legal upper hand that left householders in precarious positions when faced with troublesome or burdensome lodgers. As seen in Chapter 3 and the present chapter, householders could struggle to obtain payment for board and lodgings from unwilling lodgers, with the only route being to serve notice to leave before they became any further out of pocket. Others were forced into caring for ailing lodgers when no-one else would take responsibility for them. Moreover, when a lodger showed no inclination to take their leave, householders had little course of action to remove them from their homes, and, as well as losing autonomy over their own homes, they could lose their own lives in the worst situations. Yet it is not all a negative story. The inquest reports also provide glimpses of compassion within the householder–lodger relationship regarding the lodger's exit from the home. As well as being saddened by their moving on, lodgers could find themselves tended to by female householders in their dying days and hours.

Death also paved the way for the end of lodgings. For the lodger, the death of the householder meant moving on to new lodgings. For female lodgers, the death of the married female householder invited the possibility of promotion as the widowers sought domestic assistance. Meanwhile, the death of a lodger did not always mean seeking a new lodger to replace the deceased. Instead, for some, especially having been mainly dependent on the same lodger for many years, their death signalled a point of change in their domestic circumstances. Indeed, for some householders, the death of a lodger brought them onto the path of lodgings for themselves.

Notes

1 Antcliffe was one of the few lodgers in my sample paying for lodgings by the month.
2 *Nottinghamshire Guardian*, 22 July 1864, p. 10; TNA, RG09/2357, f. 10, p. 13, s. 55, 1861 England, Wales & Scotland Census.
3 Gillian Williamson, *Lodgers, Landlords and Landladies in Georgian London* (London: Bloomsbury Academic, 2021), pp. 145–67.
4 'Lodgers have generally the same rights and are subject to the same liabilities as other tenants. If apartments are let at so much per week, or quarter, the tenancy will be a weekly, monthly, or quarterly one, and notice to quit, unless otherwise agreed upon will be regulated by the letting as a week's notice if taken by the week, &c.' Unless, a specified length of time. Furthermore, 'The notice to quit need not be in any particular form', John Mayhall, *A Plain Guide to Landlords Tenants and Lodgers with a Collection of Useful Forms*, 3rd edition (London, 1862), pp. 9–10, 32.
5 *London Evening Standard*, 14 April 1870, p. 6.
6 Mayhall, *A Plain Guide*, pp. 21–2.

7 *Reynold's Newspaper*, 18 June 1876, p. 6; *Sydenham Times*, 27 June 1876, p. 2.

8 *Yorkshire Evening Post*, 29 August 1894, p. 4.

9 *Stockton Herald, South Durham and Cleveland Advertiser*, 16 December 1882, p. 6.
   Shortly after their departure, Brannan died from his injuries and the Neillans were arrested and charged with manslaughter. Brought before Durham's assize court, Susan was acquitted. Her husband, John, found guilty by the jury but recommended for mercy, was sentenced to eight years of penal servitude. *Stockton Herald, South Durham and Cleveland Advertiser*, 27 January 1883, p. 8.

10 *Warwick & Warwickshire Advertiser*, 4 July 1840, p. 3.

11 *Burnley Express*, 4 July 1894, p. 3.

12 *Sheffield Independent*, 12 July 1894, p. 7; *Barnsley Chronicle*, 14 July 1894, p. 8.

13 *Bromyard News*, 21 June 1900, p. 7.

14 Robert Kemp Philp, *The Dictionary of Daily Wants*, vol. 2 (London: Houlston & Wright, 1859), p. 646.

15 For example, in 1872, Jane stole and sold a shirt and shift from a neighbouring home, having been entrusted with washing for them. Know to the courts as 'an old offender', Jane was sentenced to three months with hard labour. *Exeter and Plymouth Gazette*, 8 June 1872, p. 3.

16 *Exeter and Plymouth Gazette Daily Telegrams*, 18 July 1876, p. 2; *Western Times*, 18 July 1876, p. 5.

17 Several other newspaper reports spell their surname as Whitting and, at the Old Bailey trial, he is referred to as Walter Whitting. However, for the sake of consistency, the name is given in the most detailed account of the coroner's inquest.

18 *London Evening Standard*, 8 September 1870, p. 7; *The Day's Doings*, 24 September 1870, p. 10; *Morning Advertiser*, 7 September 1870, p. 7; Old Bailey Proceedings Online, www.oldbaileyonline.org, version 8.0 (accessed 12 May 2023), September 1870, trial of THOMAS WALKER (36) (t18700919-757).

19 *Preston Chronicle*, 7 November 1846, p. 7.

20 *Burnley Express*, 29 October 1927, p. 18.

21 *Weston-Super-Mare Gazette, and General Advertiser*, 5 December 1888, p. 2; *Western Chronicle*, 14 December 1888, p. 6; *Western Gazette*, 30 November 1888, p. 7.

22 *Leigh Chronicle and Weekly District Advertiser*, 29 May 1908, 2. TNA, RG14/23246, s. 53, 1911 England, Wales & Scotland Census; TNA, RG15/18473, s. 369, 1921 England, Wales & Scotland Census.

23 *Essex Standard*, 15 April 1864, p. 6.

24 *West Briton and Cornwall Advertiser*, 29 November 1900, p. 11.

25 TNA, HO107/1951, f. 366, p. 6, s. 27, 1851 England, Wales & Scotland Census.

26 TNA, RG10/2533, f. 25, p. 1, s. 6, 1871 England, Wales & Scotland Census.

27 *Bristol Mercury*, 13 May 1876, p. 6.

28 *Woolwich Gazette*, 6 July 1888, p. 5.

29 *Chester Chronicle*, 7 May 1870, p. 6.

30 (Ipswich) *Evening Star*, 9 May 1898, p. 2.

31 TNA, RG13/1775, f. 45, p. 33, s. 218; RG13/1781, f. 125, p. 13, s. 0, 1901 England, Wales & Scotland Census.

32 *Oxford Times*, 18 August 1900, p. 5. Also see *Oxford Times*, 11 August 1900, p. 7.

33 *Reading Mercury*, 3 October 1840, p. 4; *Blackburn Standard*, 21 October 1840, p. 2.

34 Williamson, *Lodgers, Landlords and Landladies*, p. 167.

Conclusion

This book began with an army of census enumerators knocking on doors across England on the night of the 1891 census. Teetering on the thresholds, they observed over one million persons lodgings in domestic dwellings, many of those inhabited by the working class. The details they gathered on their schedules about these householders and their lodgers, however, leave us with many questions as to who, why, and how of the domestic dwelling lodging arrangement. Yet while the census enumerators remained on the front step to the working-class home, the coroners of Victorian England traversed these dwellings unhindered in their investigations, the details of which – sometimes verging on the prurient – were recorded in the many local newspapers in existence at this time. Turning to these inquest reports, I have been able to document the domestic dwelling lodging arrangement from beginning to end, and in doing so, add significantly to our understanding of household economy, gender and household dynamics, social networks, and ideas of privacy among the Victorian working class.

Long seen as the domain of widows, the inquest reports reveal that taking in lodgers was central to the economics of makeshift to a range of struggling working-class households throughout the Victorian period. Alongside widows and other female-headed households spurned or scantily supported by the Poor Law authorities, the failures of the breadwinner economy brought lodgers under the roofs of male-headed households that were unable, at certain points in the lifecycle, or – in the worst-case scenario – unwilling to support their family. However, as the inquest reports also make clear, taking in a lodger did not necessarily alleviate the male householder's financial distress nor provide the security it should have done to the female-headed householder. Lodgers who could not or would not pay placed householders in precarious positions, and while technically there were legal routes open to householders to deal with financially troublesome lodgers, they had little authority over burdensome or uncooperative lodgers. Indeed, some male heads could find their households entirely upended when their wives ran off with the lodger.

Sexual relations between female householders and their lodgers were widely disseminated in Victorian popular culture. Certainly, the inquest reports confirm the presence of sexual relationships between lodgers and the women with whom they lodged. However, when it comes to wives, widows, and other lone women and their lodgers, the inquest reports tend to tell a different story from that portrayed in comic literature and music hall. While in some cases, the male lodger fell into the stereotype of the seducer, the cases of adultery – not just those imagined by a jealous husband – between wives and lodgers that are revealed in the inquest reports suggest that the marriage they upended had already been regretted. Regardless, the male lodger was held accountable for his sins. Meanwhile, long seen as preying upon their unsuspecting male lodgers in pursuit of a replacement for their recently departed husbands, it appears more likely to be the case that widows, such as Betty Scott, were nothing if not cautious when it came to embarking on relationships with their insistent male lodgers. Indeed, their unusual position as the head of the household granted them the power to be choosy. However, such a reversal of power dynamics in the relationship was not without tensions or tragedies. Those who did come to marry their male lodgers in haste did not necessarily find a happy ending. Furthermore, where marriage was out of the question or denied, the male lodger turned to violence to gain dominance under his paramour's roof.

Many of the lodgers appearing in inquest reports do not conform to the stereotype of the lodger – the young, usually migrant male. While domestic dwelling lodgings provided many young men with a temporary home before marriage, they were also home to working-class men and women across the lifecycle. Indeed, even non-migrants – men and women of all ages and marital statuses – found themselves in domestic dwelling lodgings. For some, such as newlyweds and impoverished families, the move to lodgings was driven by the need for cheap housing. Overwhelmingly, however, the move into lodgings for many non-migrants and established residents was precipitated by the dismantling of their own family home caused by, in many cases, the death of a parent or the breakdown of a marriage. Furthermore, while many of the persons we encounter in the book lived just weeks, months or even several years as a lodger, continuing a trend from the eighteenth century, some men (and perhaps some women, though they do not appear in the inquest reports examined) spent the whole of their adult life living as lodgers in someone else's home. However, we can still only speculate whether perpetual lodging occurred through choice or circumstance for these men.

Moreover, in examining the process of finding lodgings, the inquest reports also challenge the perception of the lodger as a stranger in any sense of the word. As observed by Peter Baskerville in the Canadian census, lodgers and householders were 'familiar strangers' – not known to each other but rather sharing a common connection. However, in turning to the inquest reports, I have shown that many lodgers and householders were entirely 'familiar', with lodgings sought among workmates, neighbours, friends, and even kin at little notice. Such connections between householders and their lodgers suggest that the working class neither wanted to take in nor lodge with a stranger. Indeed, the inquest reports even revealed that those who had travelled far from their native homes in search of work did not necessarily have to turn to strangers for lodgings. Locating these connections also goes a long way to understanding how householders and lodgers often lived so comfortably cheek-by-jowl.

In the daily world of the working-class domestic dwelling lodging, the lives of householders and lodgers – particularly those who boarded – were entirely entwined at the kitchen table, around the fireside, and beyond the home. Even where the householder or lodger could retreat to their own space, leisure time was often spent in each other's company. Sociability, as well as connection, was thus a crucial component of many lodging arrangements. Indeed, to the onlooker peering through the window, the lodger was indistinguishable from others in the familial scene, both at times of cordiality and conflict. Such scenes, however, perpetuated the middle-class belief that the presence of the lodger in the working-class home signalled an absence of private family life. Yet while the working class did not adhere to nor necessarily aspire to middle-class notions of privacy, lines of separation were drawn when it came to sleeping arrangements.

As the day closed, alongside the boundary created between the outside world and the home by securing the front door, a clear delineation was drawn between householders and their lodgers. Where the lodger slept has long been a matter of speculation. Yet as the Victorian coroner's courts made their way into these nocturnal spaces to view bodies and question witnesses, they documented extensively the sleeping arrangements therein. While they found that, where necessary, a female lodger might be squeezed into the family fold or a male lodger into the bed of the male householder, what they overwhelmingly saw and heard was that lodgers were generally crowded out of one and two-roomed dwellings. Indeed, in nearly all homes, the preferred arrangement was for lodgers to sleep separately from the family with whom they lodged. Nevertheless, accommodating lodgers still meant compromises had to be made. Families accommodating lodgers could find themselves in overcrowded sleeping quarters, while lodgers – it making more economic sense to accommodate more than one – generally shared a bedroom and, in some cases, a bed with friends and strangers.

A study of domestic dwelling lodgings also significantly contributes to our understanding of the Victorian working-class economy. As well as continuing the discussion of the failings of an economy dependent on the male breadwinner's wage and the importance of the lodger's contribution to the economy of makeshift in both male and female-headed households, the inquest reports also take us into the world of everyday financial exchanges among the working classes that – had it not been for the event of a death necessitating an inquest – would have otherwise gone unrecorded. Alongside providing details of the monetary exchange for bed, board, and other services, the inquest reports reveal that the lodging exchange was not always monetarily based. As Beverley Lemire's work has shown, informal economies still played an essential role in exchanges between the working classes, particularly among women. Therefore, it is unsurprising to find in the inquest report that while men paid for their lodgings and board with cash from their weekly pay packets, women lacking financial means sought to obtain and retain lodgings by exchanging domestic services for a bed and even board. Of course, such exchanges were not entirely altruistic. While community and moral obligation played a role in such exchanges, these non-monetary exchanges were, at their core, mutually beneficial arrangements often centred around the demands of childcare and employment or, in some cases, companionship.

Eventually, however, the domestic dwelling lodging arrangement itself was served its own notice. By the early twentieth century, the lodger was no longer as ubiquitous as he or she had once been in the working-class home. Technological and societal changes in the first decades of the twentieth century meant taking in a lodger or taking up lodgings was simply no longer the necessity it had been among the Victorian working class. For those who might once have sought lodgings, improved transportation in the form of trams, buses, and bicycles enabled young people to stay at home and build up the necessary means to marry and establish a home without, as Davidoff states, spending a quarter of their wages on board and lodgings.[1]

Meanwhile, the bereaved, the sick, and the elderly, for whom the lodger had provided such a vital safety net, were increasingly able to turn to the State for support as its welfare provisions moved away from the tyranny of the Poor Law and the necessity of lodgers. For example, the Old Age Pension Act came into force in 1909; single persons over seventy received five shillings a week, while married couples received 7s. 6d., far outweighing the income generated by a single lodger.[2] In 1911, the introduction of National Insurance provided a replacement for the lodger as the short-term safety net for those families hit by the illness of the breadwinner.[3] Finally, in 1925, widows under the age of sixty-five whose husbands had paid their National Insurance contributions now received ten shillings a week in state support until eligible for an old age pension. No longer was it necessary for these bereaved women to be burdened with so many lodgers under their roof.[4]

A changing housing market and new housing policies saw lodgers elbowed out of the family home. As Davidoff discusses, owner-occupation burgeoned among the working classes in the early twentieth century, but 'building societies were more attracted to houses designed for nuclear families only', while in municipal housing, there was a coinciding clamp-down on the subletting of rooms.[5] Changing ideals also left little space for a lodger. Having found themselves in the folds of the Victorian working-class family, the lodger was cast out of its all-encompassing circle as the ideal of the nuclear family took hold.[6] Of course, some householders still found it necessary or prudent to accommodate a lodger. However, rather than being incorporated into the home, they now, as Lesley Hoskins and Rebecca Preston observed in their recent research, 'slipped unostentatiously' through the family's kitchen on their way to the lavatory.[7]

But is the lodger now making a return to the home? In her book on eighteenth-century lodgers, landladies, and landlords, Williamson remarks, 'homeowners are free to take a paying guest into their home without any regulation (other than the need to pay income tax above the tax-free allowance)'.[8] To date, however, many of these paying guests have been in the form of short holiday-type lets via online companies, such as Airbnb, where there is little, if any, interaction with the owner. Yet as the housing and financial crises collide, the lodger is beginning to return to domestic dwellings, living cheek-by-jowl once again with the householder and their families. Yet there is one distinct difference between the Victorian and the modern era: lodgers are not found in England's poorest homes, for various council and social housing policies generally prohibit their presence. Instead, lodgers – from the student to the contract worker – now live among the squeezed middle class struggling to pay their bills and mortgage.[9]

Notes

1 Leonore Davidoff, 'The Separation of Home and Work? Landladies and Lodgers in Nineteenth-and Twentieth-Century England', in Sandra Burman (ed.), *Fit Work for Women* (London: Croom Helm, 1979), pp. 91–3.

2 There were exceptions to the receipt of a pension: 'Pensions were not paid to people who had continually failed to find work; who had been in prison that last ten years; who had claimed poor relief in the last two years; or who were drunkards.' Rosemary Rees, *Poverty and Public Health, 1815–1948* (Oxford: Heinemann, 2001), p. 89.

3 Rees, *Poverty and Public Health*, p. 91.

4 S. P. Breckinridge, 'Widows' and Orphans' Pensions in Great Britain', *Social Service Review*, 1:2 (1927), 249–57.

5 Davidoff, 'The Separation of Home and Work', pp. 91–3.

6 Davidoff, 'The Separation of Home and Work', pp. 91–3.

7 Lesley Hoskins and Rebecca Preston, 'Chickens, Ducks, Rabbits, and Me Dad's Geraniums: The Use and Meaning of Yards, Gardens and Other Outside Spaces of Urban Working-Class Homes', in Joseph Harley, Vicky Holmes, and Laika Nevalainen (eds), *The Working Class at Home, 1790–1940* (Cham: Palgrave Macmillan, 2022), pp. 156–9.

8 Gillian Williamson, *Lodgers, Landlords and Landladies in Georgian London* (London: Bloomsbury Academic, 2021), p. 169.

9 Nick Harding, 'Why Live-In Lodgers Are Making a Comeback', *The Telegraph online*, 8 July 2023. www.telegraph.co.uk/money/property/buy-to-let/cost-of-living-crisis-lodgers-house-sharing-comeback/ (accessed 12 January 2024).

Bibliography

Primary sources

Printed primary sources

*Newspapers via the British Newspaper Archive (www.britishnews
paperarchive.co.uk)*
Aris's Birmingham Gazette
Ashbourne News Telegraph
Barnsley Chronicle
Batley News
Birmingham & Aston Chronicle
Birmingham Daily Post
Birmingham Journal
Birmingham Mail
Birmingham Post
Blackburn Standard
Bolton Evening News
Bradford Daily Telegraph
Bradford Observer
Barnsley Chronicle
Blackburn Standard
Bristol Mercury
Bristol Times and Mirror
Bromley & District Times
Bromsgrove & Droitwich Messenger
Bromyard News
Buckingham Advertiser
Burnley Express
Burnley Gazette
Cambridge Daily News

Cambridge Independent Press
Chelmsford Chronicle
Cheltenham Journal
Cheshire Observer
Chester Chronicle
Chester Courant
Clerkenwell News
Cornish Telegraph
The Cornwall Chronicle
County Advertiser & Herald for Staffordshire and Worcestershire
The Courier
Crewe Guardian
Daily Gazette for Middlesbrough
Daily News (London)
Day's Doings
Derbyshire Advertiser and Journal
Derbyshire Courier
Devizes & Wiltshire Gazette
East Anglian Daily Times
Eastern Morning News
Essex Herald
Essex Standard
Evening Star (Ipswich)
Exeter & Plymouth Gazette
Express (London)
Gloucester Journal
Gloucestershire Echo
Gloucestershire Chronicle
Gloucestershire Citizen
Halifax Guardian
Hampshire Advertiser
Hampshire Independent
Hartlepool Northern Daily Mail
Huddersfield Chronicle
Hull Packet
Ipswich Journal
Isleworth Echo (London)
Islington Gazette
Jackson's Oxford Journal
Kendal Mercury
Kent & Sussex Courier
Kentish Independent

Kentish Chronicle
Kentish Mercury
Kilburn Times
Lambeth & Southwark Advertiser
Leamington Spa Courier
Leeds Mercury
Leeds Times
Leamington Spa Courier
Leigh Chronicle & Weekly District Advertiser
Lincolnshire Echo
Liverpool Mercury
Lloyd's Weekly Newspaper
London Daily Chronicle
London Evening Standard
Maidenhead Advertiser
Maidstone Journal and Kentish Advertiser
Manchester Courier & Lancashire General Advertiser
Manchester Evening News
Manchester Times
Marylebone Mercury
Middlesex Independent
Morning Advertiser
Morning Chronicle
Morning Herald (London)
Morning Post
Newcastle Courant
Newcastle Journal
Norfolk Chronicle
Norfolk News
North London News
Northern Star
Northwich Guardian
Norwich Mercury
Nottingham Evening Post
Nottingham Journal
Nottinghamshire Evening News
Nottinghamshire Guardian
Oxford Chronicle & Reading Gazette
Oxford Times
Oxfordshire Weekly News
People
Preston Chronicle

Preston Herald
Reading Mercury
Reynold's Newspaper
Royal Cornwall Gazette
Runcorn Advertiser
Sheffield Daily Telegraph
Sheffield Evening Telegraph
Sheffield Independent
Shields Daily News
Shields Gazette & Daily Telegraph
Shrewsbury Chronicle
Soulby's Ulverston Advertiser & General Intelligencer
South London Press
South Wales Echo
Staffordshire Advertiser
Stockton Herald, South Durham & Cleveland Advertiser
Stroud Journal
Sun (London)
Sunderland Daily Echo
Surrey Advertiser
Surrey Comet
Sussex Advertiser
Sussex Agricultural Express
Sydenham Times
Tasmania Newspapers
The Telegraph
Todmorden & District News
Ulverston Mirror & Furness Reflector
Walsall Observer
Walthamstow and Leyton Guardian
Warwick & Warwickshire Advertiser
Wilts and Gloucestershire Standard
West Briton & Cornwall Advertiser
Western Chronicle
Western Gazette
Western Morning News
Western Times
Weston Mercury
Weston-Super-Mare Gazette & General Advertiser
Whitehaven News
Windsor & Eton Express
Woolwich Gazette
Worcester Journal

Yorkshire Evening Post
Yorkshire Evening Press
Yorkshire Post and Leeds Intelligencer

Advice and legal guides

Mayhall, John, *A Plain Guide to Landlords Tenants and Lodgers with a Collection of Useful Forms*, 3rd edition (London, 1862)

Orchard, Samuel, *Beeton's Law Book: A Practical Compendium of the General Principles of English Jurisprudence* (London: Ward Lock and Tyler, 1876)

Philp, Robert Kemp, *The Dictionary of Daily Wants*, vol. 2 (London: Houlston & Wright, 1859)

Statistical inquiries

Census of Great Britain, 1841, Enumeration Abstract, BPP 1843 XXII (496) 459

Census of England and Wales, 1901, BPP 1901 XC [Cd.616] 3

Manchester Statistical Society, *Inquiry into the Educational and Other Conditions of a District of Deansgate* (Manchester, 1864)

Manchester Statistical Society, *Inquiry into the Educational and Other Conditions of a District in Ancoats* (Manchester, 1865)

Websites and online material

British Newspaper Archive www.britishnewspaperarchive.co.uk (accessed 5 February 2024)

Findmypast www.findmypast.co.uk (accessed 5 February 2024)

FreeBMD www.freebmd.org.uk (accessed 5 February 2024)

Histpop.org www.histpop.org (accessed 21 December 2023)

Old Bailey Proceedings Online www.oldbaileyonline.org (accessed 31 October 2023)

Schürer, Kevin and Edward Higgs, Integrated Census Microdata (I-CeM), 1851–1911. [data collection]. UK Data Service. SN: 7481 (2020). DOI: 10.5255/UKDA-SN-7481-2

Secondary sources

Books and articles

Anderson, Michael, *Family Structure in Nineteenth Century Lancashire* (Cambridge: Cambridge University Press, 1971)

Anderson, Michael, 'The Social Implications of Demographic Change', in F. M. L. Thompson (ed.), *The Cambridge Social History of Britain*, Vol. 2 (Cambridge: Cambridge University Press, 1990), pp. 1–70

Baskerville, Peter, 'Familiar Strangers: Urban Families with Boarders, Canada, 1901', *Social Science History*, 25:3 (2001), 321–46. DOI: 10.1017/S0145553200012141

Beito, David T. and Linda Royster Beito, 'The "Lodger Evil" and the Transformation of Progressive Housing Reform, 1890–1930', *The Independent Review*, 20:4 (2016), 485–508

Bradbury, Bettina, 'Pigs, Cows, and Boarders: Non-Wage Forms of Survival Among Montreal families, 1861–1891', *Labour/Le Travail*, 14 (1984), 9–48.

Breathnach, Ciara, *Ordinary Lives, Death, and Social Class: Dublin City Coroner's Court, 1876–1902* (Oxford: Oxford University Press, 2022)

Breckinridge, S. P., 'Widows' and Orphans' Pensions in Great Britain', *Social Service Review*, 1:2 (1927), 249–57

Briganti, Chiara and Kathy Mezei (eds), *Living with Strangers: Bedsits and Boarding Houses in Modern English Life, Literature and Film* (London: Bloomsbury, 2018)

Bronstein, Jamie L., *The Happiness of the British Working Class* (Redwood City, CA: Stanford University Press, 2023)

Burney, Ian A., *Bodies of Evidence: Medicine and the Politics of the English Inquest, 1830–1926* (Baltimore, MD: Johns Hopkins University Press, 2000)

Churchill, David, *Crime Control and Everyday Life in the Victorian City: The Police and the Public* (Oxford: Oxford University Press, 2018)

Conley, Carolyn A., *The Unwritten Law: Criminal Justice in Victorian Kent* (Oxford: Oxford University Press, 1991)

Cooper, Di and Moira Donald, 'Households and "Hidden" Kin in Early-Nineteenth-Century England: Four Case Studies in Suburban Exeter, 1821–1861', *Continuity and Change*, 10:2 (1995), 257–78. DOI: 10.1017/S026841600000268X

Crook, Tom, 'Accommodating the Outcast: Common Lodging Houses and the Limits of Urban Governance in Victorian and Edwardian London', *Urban History*, 35:3 (2008), 414–36. DOI: 10.1017/S0963926808005713

Daen, Laurel, '"To Board & Nurse a Stranger": Poverty, Disability, and Community in Eighteenth-Century Massachusetts', *Journal of Social History*, 53:3 (2020), 716–41. DOI: 10.1093/jsh/shy117

Davidoff, Leonore, 'The Separation of Home and Work? Landladies and Lodgers in Nineteenth-and Twentieth-Century England', in Sandra Burman (ed.), *Fit Work for Women* (London: Croom Helm, 1979), pp. 64–97

Davidoff, Leonore, *Worlds Between: Historical Perspectives on Gender and Class* (Cambridge: Polity Press, 1995)

Davidoff, Leonore, Megan Doolittle, Janet Fink, and Katherine Holden, *The Family Story: Blood, Contract, and Intimacy, 1830–1960* (London: Longman, 1999)

Dennis, Richard and Stephen Daniels, '"Community" and the Social Geography of Victorian Cities', *Urban History*, 8 (1981), 7–23. DOI: 10.1017/S0963926800005265

Fraser, Derek, *A History of Modern Leeds* (Manchester: Manchester University Press, 1980)

Frost, Ginger S., *Living in Sin: Cohabiting as Husband and Wife in Nineteenth-Century England* (Manchester: Manchester University Press, 2011)

Gamber, Wendy, 'Away from Home: Middle-Class Boarders in the Nineteenth-Century City', *Journal of Urban History*, 31:3 (2005), 289–305. DOI: 10.1177/0096144204272415

Gillis, John R., *For Better, For Worse: British Marriages, 1600 to the Present* (New York: Oxford University Press, 1985)

Griffin, Emma, 'Diets, Hunger and Living Standards During the British Industrial Revolution', *Past & Present*, 239:1 (2018), 71–111. DOI: 10.1093/pastj/gtx061

Griffin, Emma, *Bread Winner: An Intimate History of the Industrial Revolution* (New Haven, CT: Yale University Press, 2020)

Hamlett, Jane, *At Home in the Institution: Material Life in Asylums, Lodging Houses and Schools in Victorian and Edwardian England* (Basingstoke: Palgrave Macmillan, 2015)

Harris, Richard, 'The End Justifies the Means: Boarding and Rooming in a City of Homes, 1890–1951', *Journal of Social History*, 26 (1992), 331–58. DOI: 10.1353/jsh/26.2.331

Harris, Richard, 'The Flexible House: The Housing Backlog and the Persistence of Lodging, 189 1–1951', *Social Science History*, 18 (1994), 31–53. DOI: 10.1017/S0145553200021441

Harrison, Brian, *Drink and the Victorians: The Temperance Question in England, 1815–1872* (Staffordshire: Keele University Press, 1994)

Heathcote, Bernard V., *Viewing the Lifeless Body: A Coroner and His Inquests Held in Nottinghamshire Public Houses during the Nineteenth Century 1828 to 1866* (Nottingham: Nottinghamshire County Council, Culture & Community, 2006)

Hewitt, Martin, 'District Visiting and the Constitution of Domestic Space in the Mid-Nineteenth Century', in Janet Floyd and Inga Bryden (eds), *Domestic Space: Reading the Nineteenth-Century Interior* (Manchester: Manchester University Press, 1999), pp. 121–41

Higgs, Edward, *Making Sense of the Census Revisited* (London: HMSO, 2005)

Hollen Lees, Lynn, *The Solidarities of Strangers: The English Poor Laws and the People, 1700–1948* (Cambridge: Cambridge University Press, 2006)

Holmes, Vicky, 'Accommodating the Lodger: The Domestic Arrangements of Lodgers in Working-Class Dwellings in a Victorian Provincial Town', *Journal of Victorian Culture*, 19:3 (2014), 314–31. DOI: 10.1080/13555502.2014.947181

Holmes, Vicky, 'Death of an Infant: Coroners' Inquests and the Study of Victorian Domestic Practice', *Home Cultures*, 11:3 (2014), 305–31. DOI: 10.2752/175174214X14035295691319

Holmes, Vicky, *In Bed with the Victorians: The Life-Cycle of Working-Class Marriage* (Cham: Palgrave Macmillan, 2017)

Holmes, Vicky, 'Pulling Back the Covers: Uncovering Beds in the Victorian Working-Class Home', in Joseph Harley, Vicky Holmes, and Laika Nevalainen (eds), *The Working Class at Home, 1790–1940* (Cham: Palgrave Macmillan, 2022), pp. 73–95

Horrell, Sara and Jane Humphries, '"The Exploitation of Little Children": Child Labor and the Family Economy in the Industrial Revolution', *Explorations in Economic History*, 32:4 (1995), 485–516. DOI: 10.1006/exeh.1995.1021

Horrell, Sara and Jane Humphries, 'Women's Labour Force Participation and the Transition to the Male-Breadwinner Family, 1790–1865', *The Economic History Review*, 48:1 (1995), 89–117. DOI: 10.2307/2597872

Horrell, Sara and Jane Humphries, 'The Origins and Expansion of the Male Breadwinner Family: The Case of Nineteenth-Century Britain', *International Review of Social History*, 42:s5 (1997), 25–64. DOI: 10.1017/S0020859000114786

Horrell, Sara, Jane Humphries, and Jacob Weisdorf, 'Beyond the Male Breadwinner: Life-cycle Living Standards of Intact and Disrupted English Working Families, 1260–1850', *Economic History Review*, 75:2 (2022), 530–60. DOI: 10.1111/ehr.13105

Hosgood, Christopher P., '"Mercantile Monasteries": Shops, Shop Assistants, and Shop Life in Late-Victorian and Edwardian Britain', *Journal of British Studies*, 38:3 (1999), 322–53. DOI: 10.1086/386197

Hoskins, Lesley, 'Stories of Work and Home in the Mid-Nineteenth Century', *Home Cultures*, 8:2 (2011), 151–69. DOI: 10.2752/175174211X12961586699720

Hoskins, Lesley and Rebecca Preston, 'Chickens, Ducks, Rabbits, and Me Dad's Geraniums: The Use and Meaning of Yards, Gardens and

Other Outside Spaces of Urban Working-class Homes', in Joseph Harley, Vicky Holmes, and Laika Nevalainen (eds), *The Working Class at Home, 1790–1940* (Cham: Palgrave Macmillan, 2022), pp. 145–69

Humphries, Jane, 'Female-headed Households in Early Industrial Britain: The Vanguard of the Proletariat?', *Labour History Review*, 63:1 (1998), 31–65. DOI: 10.3828/lhr.63.1.31

Humphries, Jane and Ryah Thomas, '"The Best Job in the World": Breadwinning and the Capture of Household Labor in Nineteenth and Early Twentieth-Century British Coalmining', *Feminist Economics*, 29:1 (2023), 97–140. DOI: 10.1080/13545701.2022.2128198

Hussey, David and Margaret Ponsonby, *The Single Homemaker and Material Culture in the Long Eighteenth Century* (Farnham: Ashgate, 2012)

Kay, Alison C., 'A Little Enterprise of Her Own: Lodging-House Keeping and the Accommodation Business in Nineteenth-Century London', *London Journal*, 28:2 (2003), 41–53. DOI: 10.1179/ldn.2003.28.2.41

Kay, Alison C., '"It buys me freedom": Genteel Lodging in Late-Seventeenth- and Eighteenth-Century London', *Parergon*, 24:2 (2007), 139–61. DOI: 10.3316/ielapa.200802523

King, Peter, *Sickness, Medical Welfare and the English Poor, 1750–1834* (Manchester: Manchester University Press, 2018)

Kesselring, K.J., 'No Greater Provocation? Adultery and the Mitigation of Murder in English Law', *Law and History Review*, 34:1 (2016), 199–225. DOI: 10.1017/S0738248015000681

Levine-Clark, Marjorie, 'From "Relief" to "Justice and Protection:" The Maintenance of Deserted Wives, British Masculinity, and Imperial Citizenship, 1870–1920', *Gender and History*, 22:2 (2010), 302–21. DOI: 10.1111/j.1468-0424.2010.01592.x

MacDonald, Michael, 'Suicide and the Rise of the Popular Press in England', *Representations*, 22 (1988), 36–55

McEwan, Joanne 'The Lodging Exchange: Space, Authority and Knowledge in Eighteenth-Century London', in Joanne McEwan and Pamela Sharpe (eds), *Accommodating Poverty: The Housing and Living Arrangements of the English Poor, c.1600–1850* (London: Palgrave Macmillan, 2011), pp. 50–68

McManus, Ruth, 'Dublin's Lodger Phenomenon in the Early Twentieth Century', *Irish Economic and Social History*, 45:1 (2018), 23–46. DOI: 10.1177/0332489318801622

Medjuck, Sheva, 'The Importance of Boarding for the Structure of the Household in the Nineteenth Century: Moncton, New Brunswick, and Hamilton, Canada West', *Histoire Sociale/Social History* 13 (1980), 207–13

Meek, Jeff, 'Boarding and Lodging Practices in Early Twentieth-Century Scotland', *Continuity and Change*, 31:1 (2016), 79–100. DOI: 10.1017/S0268416016000084

Modell, John and Tamara K. Hareven, 'Urbanization and the Malleable Household: An Examination of Boarding and Lodging in American Families', *Journal of Marriage and Family*, 35:3 (1973), 467–79. DOI: 10.2307/350582

Moring, Beatrice, 'Widows, Children and Assistance from Society in Urban Northern Europe 1890–1910', *The History of the Family*, 13:1 (2008), 110. DOI: 10.1016/j.hisfam.2008.01.005

Moring, Beatrice, 'Women, Work and Survival Strategies in Urban Northern Europe Before the First World War', in Beatrice Moring (ed.), *Female Economic Strategies in the Modern World* (London: Routledge, 2012), pp. 45–72.

Moring, Beatrice, 'Gender, Class and Lodging in Urban Finland Around 1900', *Continuity and Change*, 31:1 (2016), 47–77. DOI: 10.1017/S0268416016000102

Moring, Beatrice, 'Introduction: Lodgers in Rural and Urban Europe in the Past', *Continuity and Change*, 31:1 (2016), 1–8. DOI: 10.1017/S0268416016000072

Muller, Nadine, 'Desperately Funny: Victorian Widows & the Comical Misfortunes of Husband Hunting, *Journal of Gender Studies*, 29:8 (2020), 926–36. DOI: 10.1080/09589236.2020.181977

Peel, Mark, 'On the Margins: Lodgers and Boarders in Boston, 1860–1900', *The Journal of American History*, 72:4 (1986), 813–34 DOI: 10.2307/1908892

Perrot, Michelle, *The Bedroom*, trans. L. Elkin (New York: Yale University Press, 2018)

Perry Curtis, L., *Jack the Ripper and the London Press* (New Haven, CT: Yale University Press, c2001)

Ponsonby, Margaret, *Stories from Home: English Domestic Interiors 1750–1850* (Aldershot: Ashgate, 2007)

Rees, Rosemary, *Poverty and Public Health, 1815–1948* (Oxford: Heinemann, 2001)

Roberts, Robert, *A Ragged Schooling* (Harmondsworth: Penguin, 1997)

Ross, Ellen, 'Survival Networks: Women's Neighbourhood Sharing in London Before World War I', *History Workshop Journal* 15:1 (1983), 4–27. DOI: 10.1093/hwi/15.1.4

Steedman, Carolyn, *An Everyday Life of the English Working Class: Work, Self and Sociability in the Early Nineteenth Century* (Cambridge: Cambridge University Press, 2013)

Stone, Lawrence, *The Family Sex and Marriage in England 1500–1800* (London: Weidenfeld & Nicolson, 1977)

Strange, Julie-Marie, *Death, Grief and Poverty in Britain, 1870–1914* (Cambridge: Cambridge University Press, 2010)

Styles, John, 'Lodging at the Old Bailey: Lodgings and their Furnishing in Eighteenth-Century London', in John Styles and Amanda Vickery (eds), *Gender, Taste and Material Culture in Britain and North America, 1700–1830* (New Haven, CT: Yale University Press, 2006), pp. 61–80

Tebbutt, Melanie, *Making Ends Meet: Pawnbroking and Working-Class Credit* (Leicester: Leicester University Press, 1983)

Thane, Pat, 'Women and the Poor Law in Victorian and Edwardian England', *History Workshop*, 6 (1978), pp. 29–51

Trotter, Lesley, *The Married Widows of Cornwall: The Story of the Wives 'Left Behind' by Emigration* (Cheltenham: Humble History Press, 2018)

Vickery, Amanda, 'An Englishman's Home Is His Castle? Thresholds, Boundaries and Privacies in the Eighteenth-Century London House', *Past & Present*, 199:1 (2008), 147–73. DOI: 10.1093/pastj/gtn006

Vickery, Amanda, *Behind Closed Doors: At Home in Georgian England* (New Haven, CT: Yale University Press, 2009)

Walker, Andrew, 'Pleasurable Homes? Victorian Model Miners' Wives and the Family Wage in a South Yorkshire Colliery District', *Women's History Review*, 6:3 (1997), 317–36. DOI: 10.1080/09612029700200147

Wiener, Martin J., *Men of Blood: Violence, Manliness, and Criminal Justice in Victorian England* (Cambridge: Cambridge University Press, 2006)

Williamson, Gillian, *Lodgers, Landlords and Landladies in Georgian London* (London: Bloomsbury Academic, 2021)

Williams, Samantha, 'Earnings, Poor Relief and the Economy of Makeshifts: Bedfordshire in the Early Years of the New Poor Law', *Rural History*, 16:1 (2005), 21–52. DOI: 10.1017/S0956793304001293

Williams, Samantha K., '"I Was Forced to Leave My Place to Hide My Shame": The Living Arrangements of Unmarried Mothers in London in the Early Nineteenth Century', in Joanne McEwan and Pamela Sharpe (eds), *Accommodating Poverty: The Housing and Living Arrangements of the English Poor, c. 1600–1850* (Basingstoke: Palgrave Macmillan, 2011), pp. 191–218.

Woollard, Matthew, 'The Employment and Retirement of Older Men, 1851–1881: Further Evidence from the Census', *Continuity and Change*, 17 (2002), 437–63. DOI: 10.1017/S0268416002004381

Wright, S. J., 'Sojourners and Lodgers in a Provincial Town: The Evidence from Eighteenth-Century Ludlow', *Urban History*, 17 (1990), 14–35. DOI: 10.1017/S0963926800014334

Unpublished works

Holmes, Vicky, 'Dangerous Spaces: Working-Class Homes and Fatal Household Accidents in Suffolk, 1840–1900' (PhD thesis, University of Essex, 2012)

Index

Meek, Jeff 13n.8, 20, 48, 56, 64, 72
Mickleover Asylum 76
Moring, Beatrice 3, 40n.49, 65n.7,
  66n.14, 72, 73, 81
Muller, Nadine 117, 119
Munby, Charles 83

neighbours 44n.86, 55, 60, 61,
  80, 82, 91n.24, 99, 121,
  124, 137, 138, 142, 145,
  148n.15
see also connections; lodging
New Poor Law 20, 25, 26, 28,
  43n.82, 84, 141–2
and deserted wives 20–1
and old age 20, 145
out relief 20, 29, 32, 33, 35, 55,
  62, 126, 145
and respectability 33
and widowhood 20, 33, 38n.19,
  119, 133n.11, 146
and the workhouse 20, 28, 29,
  41n.62, 54, 55, 62, 70n.70,
  87, 141–2, 145
notice to quit 59, 120, 121,
  137–43, 147n.4
see also finances

outmigration 47, 50
overcrowding 27, 50, 91n.24,
  104–7

parental abandonment 50
Perrot, Michelle 110
Ponsonby, Margaret 5, 107
Preston, Rebecca 14n.12, 155
privacy 6, 95–9, 112n.5, 152–3

rent (householders) 19, 24, 26, 31,
  32, 34, 47, 52, 80, 81, 95,
  104, 141, 145
arrears 44n.86, 80
Roberts, Robert 124, 125
rooms 81, 104
bedroom 10–11, 59, 81, 90n.11,
  99, 100, 105–8, 110–12,
  115n.55, 120, 125, 153
cellar 106, 121

houseplace 106
kitchen 101, 105, 108, 121, 124,
  129, 140, 155
lower 105
parlour 10, 29, 98, 107–8, 141
parlour-bedrooms 98, 107
sitting room 101, 108
size of 104, 106
upper 105
yard 141
Ross, Ellen 91n.24

separation (marital) 20, 29–32,
  43, 48, 56–9, 75, 84,
  87, 122, 125, 130,
  133n.7, 144
see also desertion
sex work 51, 61
Sims, George 6
sleeping arrangements 78, 79, 81,
  104–11, 124
see also overcrowding
sleep talking 110
Society for the Prevention of
  Cruelty to Children 28
somnambulism 110
Steedman, Carolyn 76
Stone, Lawerence 130, 135n.45
Styles, John 5, 98
suicide 5, 18, 24, 32, 50–1, 57,
  62–3, 86, 97–100, 102,
  125, 130, 131, 136, 140,
  143

Thane, Pat 20
theft 27, 41n.55, 99–100, 107, 140,
  145, 148n.15
and pawing of stolen goods 99,
  100
thresholds (boundaries)
curfew 97
key 98–100
latchkey 97–9, 113n.10
knocking 82, 97–9
locks 96–100, 141
makeshift 99
lodgers' 98–100
shutting up 97

www.ingramcontent.com/pod-product-compliance
Ingram Content Group UK Ltd.
Pitfield, Milton Keynes, MK11 3LW, UK
UKHW020310280225
455658UK00008B/34